MEETING MANAGEMENT

Meeting Management

Practical advice for both new and experienced managers based on an expert's twenty years in the "wonderful wacky world" of meeting planning.

RANDY TALBOT

"...a thorough 'how-to'..." (CONTINUED ON BACK COVER)

EPM
PUBLICATIONS, INC.

Library of Congress Cataloging-in-Publication Data
Talbot, Randy.
  Meeting management: practical advice for both new and experienced managers based on an expert's twenty years in the "wonderful wacky world" of meeting planning/Randy Talbot.
    p.   cm.
  Includes index.
  ISBN 0-939009-44-7
  1. Meetings—Planning—Handbooks, manuals, etc. 2. Congresses and conventions—Planning—Handbooks, manual, etc. I. Title.
AS6.T24   1990
658.4'56—dc20   90-42543
                                                                                  CIP

Copyright © 1990 Randy Talbot
All Rights Reserved
EPM Publications, Inc., 1003 Turkey Run Road,
  McLean, VA 22101
Printed in the United States of America

Cover and book design by Tom Huestis and Eason Associates

Table of Contents

1 **INTRODUCTION** 9

2 **MEETING OBJECTIVES** 11
   Reasons for Meetings 16
   Inappropriate Reasons 17

3 **AGENDA PLANNING** 18
   Participants' and Speakers' Agendas 21

4 **ATTENDEES/PARTICIPANTS** 23
   In-House Sessions 23
   Maximizing Attendance 26

5 **COST FACTORS** 30
   List to Anticipate 33

6 **BUDGET CONSIDERATIONS** 34
   Meetings Paid For 34
   Self-Supporting Meetings 38

7 **SITE SELECTION** 45
   General 47
   Lobby 48
   Front Desk 48
   Elevators 48
   Sleeping Rooms 48
   Suites 51
   Concierge Level, VIP Tower 52
   Conference Rooms 53
   Refreshment Break Service 58
   Audio-Visual Policies 59
   Restaurants 59
   Bars/Lounges 60
   Recreational Facilities 60
   Transportation 61
   Parking 61
   Staff Attitude 62
   Location of Facility 62
   Site Inspection Report 64

8 EXHIBITS ... 71
Size of Booths ... 74
Number of Booths ... 75
Prices of Booths ... 77
Times of Day and Number of Hours ... 78
Enticements ... 78
Conflicts ... 81
Types of Booth Design ... 81
Rules and Regulations ... 82
Number of People per Booth ... 82
Exhibit Area Traffic ... 83
Electrical or Other Special Needs ... 83
Setup and Breakdown ... 84
Freight, Drayage and Storage ... 84
Security ... 85

9 NEGOTIATING FOR FACILITIES ... 86
Sleeping Rooms ... 87
　Rack Rate ... 87
　Corporate Rate ... 87
　Transient Rate ... 87
　Group Rate ... 87
　Shoulder Season ... 88
　High and Low Seasons ... 88
　Government Rate ... 88
　SMURF ... 88
　Category of Room (Single, Double, etc.) ... 89
　Suites ... 89
　Concierge Level ... 90
Conference Rooms ... 90
　Rounds ... 90
　Classroom Style ... 90
　Schoolroom ... 91
　Theater ... 91
　Hollow Square ... 91
　Reception ... 91
Profit Centers ... 92
　Sleeping Rooms ... 92
　Meals ... 97
　Meeting Space ... 100
Bargaining ... 101

10 ETHICS AND "FREEBIES" 103
    FAM Trips 104
    Site Inspection Trips 105
    Incentive Trips or Prizes 106
    Door Prizes 107
    Personal Favors 107
    No Shows 108

11 MATERIALS DEVELOPMENT 110
    Advertising Committee 112
    Program Committee 113
    Exhibit Committee 114
    Awards Committee 115
    Social Committee 116
    Oversight Committee 117
    "TO DO" List 119
    Checklist of Items to be Packed 120

12 TRAVEL LOGISTICS 121
    Getting There 121
    In and Around 125

13 PERIPHERAL ACTIVITIES 127

14 SOCIAL EVENTS 130

15 SPEAKERS/VIPs 140

16 LAST MINUTE CRUNCH 145
    Sleeping Rooms 146
    Meeting Rooms 146
    Peripheral Functions 146
    Missed Handouts 147
    Weather 147
    Strikes 148
    Speaker Illness 148
    Special Meals 148
    Meal Guarantees 149
    Function Timing 149
    Lost Registration Fees 150

17 ON-SITE MANAGEMENT 152

18 BILLING AND PAYMENT 160
    Sleeping Rooms 161
    Banquet and Other Function Charges 162
    Last Minute Charges 162
    Package Prices 162
    Wording of 163
    Payment Details 163

19 CONFERENCE EVALUATION 165
    Participant Reactions 165
    Achieving Objectives 167
    Evaluate Process 168

1

Introduction

▱ *MEETING MANAGEMENT* presents a condensation of the learning I have acquired from over twenty years' experience of meeting disasters and successes. When I began this profession, there were no organizations of professional meeting planners or college courses in conference management to help me avoid some of the potential pitfalls awaiting the unwary. As a result, many of the things I now know I must do I know from not doing them at some time and subsequently suffering the consequences.

This book will ease your way into the wonderful wacky world of meeting planning. I do not intend to scare you away from the field, although the myriad details you must master and remember to be successful may at first seem intimidating. I once read that meeting planners were one of the least paid but most satisfied groups of professionals in America. I believe this to be true, at least for the satisfaction part. What's more, the field is changing. There are now professional organizations of meeting planners, such as the Society of Government Meeting Planners and Meeting Planners International. A few courses in meeting planning or conference management are now taught in colleges and even a few (entirely too few in my view) fields of study are devoted to this subject. In addition, there are several trade magazines that give tips on meeting planning and keep planners abreast of new developments—such as taxes, new convention centers, etc.—that affect meeting management.

All these changes are for the good. Salaries are now better, and there is a heightened awareness on the part of top management of the importance of meeting planning to the overall success of an enterprise. Salaries of meeting planners range from the low $20,000s to $75,000, depending on experience and the types and numbers of meetings planned. It should be emphasized that the higher salaries are for jobs that include meeting planning as part of a larger job, one in which meeting planning is only one of the skills needed to be a senior manager.

I have always found the meeting planning responsibilities of my various jobs over the years to be the most stimulating, challenging and rewarding aspects of my worklife. At the same time, I have never held a job with the title of "Conference Manager" or "Meeting Planner". You will find these duties exist in training offices, in administrative offices, in line offices and almost anywhere else you can think of. The point is that someone has to plan meetings because it is and will continue to be necessary for people to come together to discuss things. If meeting planning is something you enjoy, step forward and offer to do it for your organization. It's an opportunity to offer a service to your company, to gain recognition for yourself and to have fun. What more can you ask of a job?

I owe thanks to my family for putting up with me during this labor of love and for proofreading my amateur typing and sometimes less-than-perfect grammar. Many thanks also to my many mentors in the industry who have taught me, and continue to teach me, all I know.

2

Meeting Objectives

▷ So you're going to have a meeting (conference). Why? Let me restate that—*why??*

The most crucial question to be answered in planning a meeting or conference is just that; why are we doing this? Unfortunately, it is also the question that is often not asked because it is assumed that everyone knows why this meeting is being held. It's *the annual meeting!* We do this meeting every year at this time. Fine, but why? What would happen if we didn't do this meeting this year, or if we changed the time of year, or if we changed the duration, design, cast of characters, etc.? In other words, why are we doing this meeting, and what do we hope to accomplish by it?

We find quite often that meeting planners or managers of programs (sometimes both) are criticized for conducting a poor meeting when, in fact, there was no way they could have succeeded because there was no reason for a meeting in the first place. Or there may have been a legitimate reason for a meeting, but it was not clearly understood; so the meeting plan did not contribute to the accomplishment of the goal.

Don't get me wrong. As the planner of thousands of meetings over nearly a twenty-year period, I am a strong believer in the value of face-to-face discussion of issues and the both formal and informal interchange that can occur in such a setting. But the failure to clearly define the goals of the meeting *as the first step* in planning will only cause you grief.

Another common problem is the failure, for bureaucratic reasons, to be willing to define the *real* reason for meeting. We need to have this expenditure look good in case someone is watching us or reviewing our notes, so we define or display the "business" reasons only and fail to admit what is often just as important as a goal: the social reasons—developing camaraderie, feeling like members of a team, building morale, or just dispelling loneliness. Many organizations such as Mary Kay and others, who utilize a work force of largely home-based workers, have long recognized the value of social events at conferences. That is about the only time when these "loners" can recognize that they have colleagues who share the same frustrations (and solutions) as they have. The same need for socializing applies to government meetings and to businesses of all types, but it is not easy to put these "soft" goals on display for all to see. As a result, the agenda does not allow room for golf outings, volleyball contests, etc., and the participants go away tired and bored rather than rejuvenated and motivated to work for an organization that values them as individuals as well as widget producers.

So how do you go about accomplishing this basic but difficult task? First, by being brutally honest with yourself. Are you, as a meeting planner, hanging on to this big meeting because it keeps you occupied for three months a year so you can avoid other tasks that are less fun? If you can answer no to that question, chances are there are real reasons to at least consider the meeting. Now you have to get those who are the principals (program managers, prime participants, etc.) to be honest with themselves and with you. If there is a combination of business and social reasons for meeting, say so, if only in private. If the primary goal is one-way communication of new information, fine. Don't waste time pretending there is an "open discussion" because that won't do what you want done. If the need is to exchange ideas, make sure you don't give in to a plenary session of 200, with floor microphones so "everyone has a chance to speak." The result of that design will be an audience for the loquacious and missed input from the quiet members of the group, along with the consequent frustrations and missed opportunities for real exchange.

My approach is to ask, "If we succeed, what will we come away with? What will we able to measure, to prove to the boss that we did accomplish what we said we would? What will be the product of this meeting?" If the response is that you just want to discuss ideas, and that you don't need to have a concrete result, perhaps you need to have an exchange of papers instead of a meeting. Or maybe you should exchange papers and then have a meeting to choose among alternatives presented in the papers.

In the field of training, the approach is to ask trainers to complete the phrase, "Participants will be able to _____." Insert in the blank an action that can be observed. "Understand" cannot be observed, but "explain three reasons for" can demonstrate an understanding, so you know you have gotten your point across. This same approach, while resisted by some, can be applied to the development of agendas for meetings and conferences. If the presentation or event does not contribute to the accomplishment of a previously agreed upon goal, either take it out or redefine the meeting goals so you know where it fits.

There are probably as many good reasons for having meetings as there are types of meetings and types of organizations. It is only when the wrong reason gets tied to the wrong organization or meeting design that we run into problems of ineffective meetings. This, of course, presupposes that the meeting planner knows enough about the organization to recognize what is a bonafide reason for meeting or meeting goal (interchangeable terms) and to avoid being trapped into a mistake. Being an inside planner helps, but outside consultants who have enough experience with meetings can also recognize faulty goal descriptions. One effective procedure is to watch for those speeches or speakers who seem to creep into the agenda design when they appear to have no relation to the stated meeting goal. If the *"boss"* wants to speak when it doesn't serve the meeting goal, don't take the heat for saying no to the boss, but make the one(s) with whom you are working on the meeting redefine the meeting goal so the speech is serving it. If they can't do it and you still can't avoid the boss's speech, at least there will be general agreement that you all have created a problem in terms of meeting design. (You can sometimes use this ploy: have the boss make a speech at dinnertime. It doesn't interrupt the "hard" agenda as much, and if it's irrelevant to the purpose of the meeting, if the dinner is good enough, it won't affect the meeting as much.)

Appendix 1 at the end of this chapter lists some possible good and poor reasons for having a meeting. Use them if they help. Remember that all kinds of reasons are *ok* as long as they are goals that can in fact be accomplished in a meeting atmosphere.

In some, perhaps many, cases there are multiple goals or reasons for having a meeting. This is fine. Sometimes problems arise, however, when the goals are contradictory or so different that it is difficult to accomplish one without jeopardizing the other. For example, you might have one goal to build morale and another goal to explain the necessity for everyone to take a pay cut. It is no easy task to put together a meeting that will accomplish both of these goals! If faced with such "at odds" goals, try to take a real hard look at one or more of them to see if one can be accomplished through a medium other than a meeting. Perhaps the pay cut could best be explained through a memorandum or letter, leaving the coast clear to try to build morale at a meeting. Another consideration should be the feasibility of accomplishing both goals right away. If you announce a pay cut through a letter and then bring everyone together for a meeting, it might be brought to your attention that the pay cut could have been smaller if you hadn't wasted money on a meeting. Maybe morale building will have to wait.

Not all conflicting goals are that extreme, of course. You can have some good news and bad news at the same meeting if you structure your agenda correctly. Remember the primary reason you need to spend time examining goals is that, properly defined, your goals will more or less dictate your agenda design, type of facility needed, and a host of other details needed for a successful meeting.

In my experience, the most common mistake made in defining goals is to say something like, "We just want to discuss the issue, it doesn't need to be decided right now." If no decision is needed, why is a discussion to be held? If you want input, try to get it in writing. If you aren't ready to address an issue, discussion may lead only to frustration. If you dig deep enough, you will usually find there is a reason behind the apparently poorly stated goal, perhaps one the manager or meeting conductor is unwilling to "publish". Again, I'm not suggesting you need to make public all reasons or goals; we all have our "hidden agenda" items. You, as a meeting planner, however, can only help if you know what these goals are. This means you have to earn the trust of those with whom you are working, assuring them that their reasons or goals will be kept private if they so wish. The point should be made, however, that if the goals, or even some of them, can be made public, they should be. Inform your meeting participants of the reason(s) for the meeting, whenever possible, as far in advance as you can. This helps to get the right people there prepared to address the issue.

To sum up with a couple of "homely homilies," it's not "Ready, fire, aim," but "Ready, aim, fire". Or, "We don't know where we're going, but we're making good time." Take time to define goals. Believe me, you'll save time later and have much better meetings (and probably fewer meetings, shorter meetings, and less expensive meetings as well).

APPENDIX—CHAPTER 2
Appropriate Reasons for Meetings

1. To exchange ideas on procedures, problems, resolutions; to share information.
2. To teach. (But please note that not all training should be done in meetings. Some is better done through readings, manuals, tape recordings, movies, etc.)
3. To develop ideas for new procedures, plans, programs.
4. To obtain feedback on tests, project progress, etc. (Often can be done, as well, or better, in writing.)
5. To announce (and explain) major new initiatives, products or policies.
6. To solve ad hoc issues or problems (turnover, misunderstandings, priority issues, etc.).
7. To celebrate a successful year.

8. To vent feelings (therapeutic reasons).
9. To reward top performances.
10. To have fun together.
11. To show off a new facility.

Inappropriate Reasons for Meetings

1. To continue previous practice of having one per year (or one per X years, etc.).
2. To explain things that can be explained better in writing.
3. To provide one-way communication.
4. To set policy outside appropriate channels.

3

Agenda Planning

✏️ Now that you have your goals firmly established (you *didn't* skip Chapter 2 did you?), it's time to plan the agenda. For me, a meeting or conference should be approached as an important event, even if it involves only a couple of days and a relatively small number of people. When you begin to look at the cost of meetings, which we will do in a later chapter, you will soon see that such careful planning is well worth the effort.

In my career, the most frequently made mistake I have seen (and made), is to cram too much into a given time frame. We decide we will meet for three days, then we see what we can accomplish in that time frame. Absolutely backwards! First we should see what we need to accomplish, then make sure there is adequate time allotted to do that. If, after doing this, we determine there is still time available within the day, week or whatever outside limit may be applicable, we can consider other possible goals or activities.

Once you get into the trap of a fixed time frame, particularly in an organization where several different groups or sub-units want to accomplish different things, you find yourself being asked to cut down on Joe's time so Harry can squeeze in a short "discussion" (usually means lecture) on _____. Non-meeting planners never seem to think their topic will take as long as it does, particularly if a discussion is involved. A lecture or slide show can be fairly accurately timed, but a free-flowing discussion can go on and on—and on—and on. It's a mistake to cut off meaningful dialogue, but it's also a mistake to let it run on after all points have been made just because some "motormouth" needs to vent his or her expertise. The size of the group needs to be considered in timing a discussion. If, for example, you want to hear a brief report from each of eight participants, remember that "brief" means different things to different people and that there will be some down time in transition from speaker to speaker, particularly if handouts or visual aids are being used in the presentations. Perhaps as long as an hour will be needed for a "short status report" from each of eight people. Remember, that's only 7½ minutes each.

Here are several basic general rules to be followed in setting up an agenda.

1. An agenda should flow. It should follow a logical sequence. This helps concentration, avoids questions that are best kept until a later topic, and increases learning or retention of the material covered. If it appears to be an unrelated hodge-podge of topics, without any apparent connection, participants become confused or bored or both.

2. It is important to begin the agenda with a formal introduction to the meeting, one in which the presenter gives the participants a "road map" of how the session will flow, what topics will be covered in what sequence, and *very briefly* what each topic listed entails. Housekeeping details, such as meal

times, location of rest rooms and so on should also be covered here. It is necessary to cover these items to make the participants feel as comfortable as possible and able to focus on the content of the meeting. A point often overlooked is that you will definitely need to repeat at least part of what is said in this introduction, because for some reason people do not hear very well what is said at the very beginning of the meeting. Probably it has something to do with "settling in".

3. If you have some inactive or passive segments (lectures, slide shows, etc.) keep them to the morning hours if at all possible. Save the active items (workshops, brainstorms, question and answer sessions) for the afternoon. And *never, never, never* show a movie immediately after lunch, (unless, of course, your group is all five-year-olds and it's nap time). The combination of full stomachs, little exercise and dark rooms is deadly to alertness.

4. If possible, try to end the session on an up note. Remember that a meeting should be an event. You would like it to be remembered fondly and to send participants away with a good feeling. I had one boss who always saved the "zinger" for the last item, because she didn't want this lecture she planned to ruin the rest of the meeting. So she hoarded it until last, then sent everyone away with a sour taste for the whole event. After a few meetings like this, anticipation of the ending zinger ruined the whole meeting anyhow. If you have something negative to lay down, get it over with and follow it with an up. Remember when your mother gave you medicine followed by juice or candy or something to make you forget the medicine? Same principle.

5. If possible, encourage participants to contribute to the agenda design. While you know what you want to cover, you don't know if it will meet their needs until you ask them. If you

cannot accommodate all requested agenda items, say so and see if they can be addressed another way (telephone call, letter or private conversation during the conference off-hours).

6. Publish the final agenda prior to the meeting. Let your participants know in advance what the coverage will be so they can come prepared. If tools or materials are needed, such as calculators or manuals, tell them so they come "armed".

7. Have two agenda versions, one for participants, with somewhat vague time-lines on it, and another for meeting presenters, with both beginning and ending times of each topic listed. This allows you to keep time controls without introducing that uneasy feeling that happens when the entire group knows someone is running beyond his allotted time. A brief example of two agenda versions is given here:

PARTICIPANTS' AGENDA

9:00 A.M.	Opening session on accomplishments
	Coffee
	Reports from committees
	Lunch

SPEAKERS' AGENDA

9:00 A.M.	Opening session on accomplishments
9:45 A.M.	Coffee break
10:15 A.M.	Reports from committees
11:45 A.M.	Reports concluded, break for lunch

8. Try to schedule breaks at roughly halfway through each session, morning and afternoon, but don't get so locked into break-timing that you break into a presentation at an inopportune time. One ploy you can use, by the way, is to schedule your long-winded speakers so that they should end their presentation

at either coffee break or lunchtime. The group's discomfort level works better as a timing device than any meeting manager's hand signals.

9. Never schedule a topic (other than introductions) for a segment of time as short as 15 minutes. If the issue is worth listing on the agenda, it should take longer than 15 minutes to adequately cover it. If it won't take that long, try to combine it with another topic as a subheading. Having short, chopped-up topics listed on the agenda causes uneasiness on the part of participants and usually means you will be running behind your plan.

10. List breaks for less time than you really intend for them to be. No one returns from break early, generally late. If you plan to serve refreshments in the meeting room, don't think it's unnecessary to schedule breaks. People still need to stretch, use the bathroom, have a smoke, or meet a variety of other needs. If you don't schedule time for them to do this, their concentration will be disrupted trying to figure out when to leave the ongoing session to do what they need to do.

11. If you have some flexibility in terms of filling complete days (meeting lasts only 1½, 2½ days, for example), remember to think about hotel check-in, check-out policies, travel plans, etc., and schedule accordingly. Generally it is easier to begin a meeting in the morning and end it at noon than it is to begin in the early afternoon and end at the end of the day. You also have the advantage of starting the meeting with all participants fresh, rather than with some who are tired from travel problems.

4

Attendees/Participants

▶ In this chapter, I address two different basic types of meetings. The first is the meeting that deals with "in-house" staff; those who are part of the organization, or for some other reason are expected or required to attend. This meeting requires no selling. In fact part of your job may be to eliminate some prospective attendees in order to accomplish what you need to do. The second is the meeting or conference that you *want* people to attend but they don't necessarily want to, or perceive that they need to attend. This meeting obviously requires some "selling", and the strategies used to determine attendance at this type of function are different from, sometimes diametrically opposed to, the process used for the first meeting.

IN-HOUSE SESSIONS
To discuss the "in-house" meeting first let us assume that you have your meeting objectives and agenda all set. The next logical step is to decide who should attend your carefully planned func-

tion. Often, of course, it doesn't follow this sequence. Instead, you are presented with a list of participants and asked to figure out what to say to them. When this happens, be aware that you are working "out of sync" with good meeting planning strategy. You are being asked to invent a goal (read excuse) for a group of people to accomplish since they are going to be in town, rather than bringing a specific group of people together to work on a specific goal.

This is not to say that there cannot be legitimate reasons found for an established group to meet, but it's much easier to be faced with inappropriate meeting objectives when you get out of sequence like this.

So if you are lucky enough to be able to work in sequence, how should you proceed? There are several conditions that need to be addressed, some cultural, some budget based, and some such practical issues like availability. Obviously you need someone who is competent to address the issues under consideration. This does not always mean, however, that you need, or even should have, *the* expert on the subject. If the session is a training session for people entirely new to the subject, it's entirely possible that the expert will talk over their heads, or not understand their lack of background or their starting point, thus resulting in a missed opportunity. A more appropriate choice of speaker in this instance might be a member of the staff who, while knowledgeable on the subject, has more common ground with the trainees, such as remembering how it felt to be ignorant on the subject.

Another consideration should be how many speakers you need on one basic subject. It may be possible for one person to cover the entire agenda, but for reasons both of speaker fatigue and listener attention span, it may be better to vary the presentations by using more than one speaker.

In some organizations it is the rule that only one person

from each unit may attend the meeting. This delegate is then expected to bring back the experience and share it with others in the unit. While this approach may sometimes be appropriate, blind adherence to this dictum limits the organization's input to issues under discussion. Another problem, of course, is what is known as filtering. Any reporter, no matter how good, puts priorities on things to be shared, based on personal attitude, background, bias, perceptions on what the group wants to hear, etc. This "filters out" some things, meaning less than full reporting on the meeting. In some cases this is acceptable, in others it's not. The cost-benefit balance of sending one or more participants to a session needs to be considered. It's easy to measure the cost, not always so easy to determine the benefit. In some instances it may be more beneficial to the organization to send more than one participant so that they can share the experience and the learning back on the job.

Another rule some organizations have is that unless you are on the agenda you can't go. This, of course, is intended for meetings that are supposed to be discussions among colleagues. However, this policy sometimes leads to presentations put on the agenda only so that someone who wants to go can do so—presentations essentially useless to the meeting's real objectives.

Prerequisites, in the case of training meetings, can be an effective measure for determining appropriate attendees. If you haven't mastered X, you can't possibly understand Y, so you must study X before you can go to a session on Y.

Another consideration, which, unfortunately, is often employed, is the location of the meeting. If participation is voluntary, you will have a much larger crowd in a nice location than you will in a location that is seen as mundane or undesirable. One way to avoid this is to develop the list of participants before the location is selected or announced. This is not always practical but is a method to try if you find yourself with participants who you believe are there for the wrong reasons.

The size of the group must also be considered. If you want to make decisions in a working session, you cannot expect to accomplish much if the group size is too large. (Maybe this is why Congress has so much trouble making decisions?) If it is necessary for more people to attend than your meeting design can accommodate, consider having multiple sessions, or plenary sessions for part of the agenda, and breakouts where needed to accomplish certain objectives. Conversely, if you cannot assemble all the key players to work on a problem, the decisions reached may not be appropriate.

MAXIMIZING ATTENDANCE

As I said at the beginning of this chapter, there are different types of meetings, requiring different strategies for developing a list of participants. Let's talk now of the meeting where you want to maximize attendance but the potential participants need to be convinced to go. The first difference to be noted is that the rule on attractive location needs to be reversed. Rather than withholding the location of the session, or avoiding a "nice" place, you want to make the nice location known to as many potential participants as you can, as early as you can.

A second basic point is to design the agenda to meet the needs and desires of the potential audience. You can't preach to an empty hall, so you may as well face up to the possibility that the agenda you may want will not bring you the audience you need. You need to find out, early in the game, what the interests of the group are and build those into the agenda. Then you have to sell not the features of your meeting but the benefits of attendance. Don't say, for example, "We will cover the basics of how to cook a steak," but something more like, "you will leave this meeting knowing how to wow your guests with your steak."

Advance notice of the meeting is important, as is the timing of that notice. You may have to do two or three mailings to your audience, spaced not so far apart as to allow the meeting to fall from their minds, but not so close together that you end up nagging them and turning them off. First notice, depending on how far recipients have to travel and how busy their calendars are, may need to be mailed as much as six months in advance. You need to start from the finish line and back up to your first mailing. By that I mean figure out when you absolutely need to know who's coming, either for the hotel's cut-off date, or for planning catered functions, and plan your mailings in reverse so you don't get caught. Generally speaking, response to a mailing comes within two to three weeks or not at all. So if you need a room list one month in advance, your last mailing might go out seven weeks ahead of the planned conference date.

If you have exhibit booths to sell, speakers to find and get commitments from, and such, you need to begin the process long before mailing your first notice to potential "customers" of the event. Your agenda should be nearly final when you do your first customer mailing, so you might need to begin the process months, (sometimes years) ahead. One consideration, for example, is that booth buyers (your exhibitors) need to put you into their advertising or marketing budget on an annual basis, so you want to make sure you don't miss potential sales by being too late in that process.

One point on which I tend to disagree with some of my colleagues is whether to have the registrants respond to you or to the hotel, or separately to each. I like to get the whole response, because it gives me more information of who's coming when, as opposed to just knowing who will be there for part of the session. (They may miss the opening reception, and I can save $15-25 per person.) Another benefit of this approach is that it's easier for the participant; they only have to fill out one form, or make one telephone call instead of two. On the negative side, it's more work for me, and if the hotel staff is efficient, they can supply me with reservations data on a weekly basis, so I will have the same information without the work. Also, if reservation changes are needed, or if upgrades or different classes of room are involved, it may be better to have the participants deal directly with the hotel. However, for small meetings at least, I still prefer to be in the middle, getting response data from the participants and feeding it to the hotel. The hotel, by the way, generally prefers to get a rooming list, so you might use that as a bargaining chip when negotiating rates or services.

Another aspect of both "in-house" meetings and those for which you need to sell attendance is that of guests, be they spouses or other. Do you intend to have a spouse program? If not, are spouses going to be allowed to attend some of the official functions, such as receptions or dinners? If the answer is no, you don't need to concern yourself about getting counts of guests. If the answer is yes, they will be welcome at some events, then you need to know numbers so you won't over or under pay for the functions. If you plan to have a spouse program then you're dealing with a whole different kind of meeting. Go back to the chapter on agenda design and apply the principles there with your guests in mind. Remember that the days of spouses being wives are gone. You need spouse or guest programs that have appeal for both sexes. If children will attend, you may have to return to the agenda design chapter a third time to set up another flow of events for entertaining them while your delegates are working.

One way for you to avoid getting the last-minute blues (from those who won't make up their minds until the last minute) is to offer early registration bonuses. A late registration fee has a negative connotation and is not usually a good marketing technique. An early bonus might mean a discount on the fee, or it could be something like a chance at an upgrade to a suite for the conference. This particular ploy is one that I like because it gives the individual a chance for a "prize", which is always more fun than a dollar savings, and it doesn't have to cost you anything because you can use your quota of free rooms to upgrade your winner. More about this when we discuss negotiations.

An issue that is often overlooked is early departure. Once you get your participants there, you assume they will stay until the last waltz is played. This assumption can end up costing you a pile of money. We once had, for example, a 40 percent drop-off from the Saturday evening banquet to the Sunday brunch. We mistakenly assumed that those who had been there Saturday evening would be there on Sunday morning. What we forgot was that about half the participants were not in residence at the hotel. They made a choice not to give up their Sunday just for a brunch, even though the registration fee included the brunch cost. This miscalculation cost us several hundred dollars because our guarantee was for the high number. Although I discuss conference planning tasks in separate chapters in this book, you can't really operate successfully without keeping details like meal counts in mind as you plan your agenda and spouse events. You must remember to have an accurate count not just for the conference, but for all events at the conference.

5

Cost Factors

Meetings cost money, an elemental fact that should come as no surprise to anyone. But how much do they cost, and what kinds of costs are entailed in holding a meeting? Which costs should be minimized, which are worth splurging on, and which are the same whether or not the meeting is held?

Some of the costs are obvious. If participants are required to travel away from their normal worksite, for example, there are travel costs. These include airfare, hotel costs (if an overnight stay is required), meals, ground transportation to and from airports, parking fees, miscellaneous expenses such as tips, telephone calls, etc.. They also include costs for the meeting room, coffee breaks, audio-visual equipment rentals, service charges, and possibly a whole host of events such as receptions, dinners, banquets and related social events. Other possible fees are for outside speakers, for upgrades in accommodations for VIPs, for preparation and shipping of materials to be handed out at the meeting and for taxes on most or all of the above.

Other costs include salaries of those attending, although it can be argued that these costs should not be considered because they would occur whether or not the meeting were held. The only circumstance, in my opinion, when salary costs should not be considered is when it can be assumed that the participants would not otherwise have been doing anything productive. This is not wholly a facetious statement. There are times when a group cannot be productive until properly trained. In fact they may be destructive rather than productive, a factor that is all too often not considered. As the old bromide goes, "We can't afford to do it right the first time, but we can pay to have it corrected several times."

A cost that is sometimes ignored is the cost in salary time required to prepare for the meeting. Agenda planning, site selection, and all the rest do take time and cost money. All the more reason to do it right, because lack of preparation will surely mean a less than optimum meeting.

Not all of these costs need to be calculated or justified every time you plan a meeting, but they should be in the back of your mind. If no other purpose is served by knowing the true cost of the meeting, you may be able to scare someone into doing a proper job of planning and preparing for a meeting, instead of just expecting it to happen.

Other categories of cost relate to alternatives, such as holding the meeting in another city, or within commuting distance or in a location where some participants will stay overnight and some will commute. While the latter may seem to be less costly, the cost savings should be balanced against the loss of time for interaction if all participants are together overnight. The meeting times may span eight hours, but many more hours are available for informal interaction—more like 16, even assuming a full eight hours for sleep. Thus you may double the interaction time at a fairly low cost if the meeting is "off site".

Some cities are considerably more expensive than others, both in hotel costs as well as for food and related expenses. As an example, New York City hotel rates are probably close to double what you might find in Des Moines. Chicago is more expensive than Milwaukee. Even within a metropolitan area costs vary; San Francisco, for instance, will cost you more than Oakland or San Mateo. In most cases, downtown hotels cost more than suburban properties. These variables should be factored into the decision-making process. Another cost difference exists within the same city, that for conference facilities. Room rates vary widely, of course, as does quality of the facility. Even if, however, the room rates are the same or similar, food and other costs can be quite different. Thus you may want to consider the make-up of your group when choosing a facility because the "best" hotel may be uncomfortable for them.

Still other differences in cost fluctuate according to the seasons of the year. Minneapolis in the winter costs less than it does in the summer, while the opposite is true in Phoenix. If you have flexibility as to choosing days of the week when you meet, you may be able to save money in a downtown property by meeting on weekends, or in a resort property by meeting mid-week.

The costs of any meeting, within the bounds of reason, are negotiable. The events you include, where you have them, when you have them. who does them for you,—all are open for consideration and alternate pricing. We will go into more detail on this in the chapter on negotiating, but it is important to note here that being aware of the various categories of costs, and that you can impact almost all of them, will go a long way toward helping you to carry off a better meeting within your budget.

As an aid in developing cost factors for your meetings, here is a list, assuredly not all-inclusive, of some costs to anticipate:

Travel
- air
- ground
- local (cabs, limousines, buses)
- parking

Salaries
- participants
- speakers
- planners
- on-site help
- time for material development

Rooming
- different categories of rooms
- suites
- VIP (speakers, others)
- single vs. double
- taxes (watch out here!)
- service charges (telephones, in-room movies)

Meals
- breakfasts
- lunches
- dinners
- meal prices for individuals
- coffee breaks
- receptions
- beverage costs and options

Meeting Costs
- conference room costs
- break-out room costs
- setup fees
- exhibit space
- labor charges
- registration space
- audio-visual equipment charges
- storage fees
- equipment hookup fees (telephones, computers)

Materials
- development costs
- printing
- mailing
- freight charges
- film costs
- royalties for use of copyrighted materials
- rental costs for films, videos
- folders, badges, notepads

Budget Considerations

▱ At some point in the development of your meeting, you must undertake the onerous task of figuring out how to pay for it. Again we have two basic approaches: (1) to have a budget devoted to the meeting and pay all the costs from that budget, or (2) design the meeting to be basically or partially self-supporting, or even money-making. We will discuss the easier one first, the development of a meeting budget.

PAID FOR
This is a fairly straight-forward task, requiring only a fair idea of the number and size of your meetings for a given period of time (typically a year), and the ability to make reliable estimates of all types of costs involved in those meetings. Having said that, however, there are always complications. You have to approach each category of cost separately, as follows:

    1. LODGING AND MEALS span a very wide range of possible costs, depending on the quality of facility and service you choose

to pay for, or can pay for. In developing a budget, you must essentially choose the level of expenditure that is right for your organization, then try to live within that level in your planning and site negotiations.

2. AUXILIARY FOOD FUNCTIONS, such as coffee breaks and receptions, offer a wide latitude of possibilities, and a necessary choice as to the level of expenditure that should be made. Once the type of service you want has been chosen it's a relatively simple matter to estimate quantities needed times price to reach a budget. There is less variation among hotels for auxiliary food costs than there is in room costs, but the range of possibilities is still wide.

3. AUDIO-VISUAL NEEDS depend on what kind of equipment you will need, for how long, and with how much labor support. Audio-visual costs are often considered a given expenditure, in that the in-house supplier of these services is assumed to be the best one to use. In fact using in-house staff can cost you a significant amount of money without necessarily increasing the quality of service you receive. The reason is that in-house contractors can be paying the hotel a commission of up to 40 percent, an amount you won't have to pay if you use a service which is not in-house. Depending on the complexity of your needs, it is often unnecessary to have a technician on-site, so an off-site contractor should be used. In some cases, hotels (or their labor unions) will not allow you to bring in audio-visual services from outside, but you should definitely explore this option.

4. TRANSPORTATION is one of the largest ticket items in your meeting budget and one of the most frustrating to deal with. My approach, quite frankly, has been to avoid it whenever possible by having the travel costs estimated on the basis of some standard algorithm, regardless of where the travelers are coming

from—say $300 round-trip for each one, regardless of time or embarkation point. This approach isn't as crazy as it sounds if you have ever tried to figure out how much it costs to go to two alternative destinations. I recently found, for example, that a flight clear across the country cost me only $10 more than one half-way across. The policy issue that does need to be addressed from the start is the type of flights or fares to be allowed. Will first class be the mode of travel, will full-coach fare be allowed, or will super-saver or 30-day non-refundable tickets be required? The choice can easily make a difference of more than 300 percent in your total transportation costs.

A secondary transportation cost, much less costly and difficult, is ground transportation. Once your participants reach the meeting city they have to get to and from the hotel. (And don't forget similar costs in the city of origin/return.) Probably the least expensive mode of reliable travel is the airport limousine service normally offered at major airports. Some hotels near airports, of course, offer free van service, which normally is quite satisfactory. Other modes of transport, such as taxi or rental car, are usually much more expensive. In some cases, however, car or taxi pooling can actually save money. Also, when the conference site is quite far from the airport, say 50 miles or so, it can be both cheaper and more satisfactory to arrange for rental cars for participants.

5. MATERIALS are sometimes ignored or discounted because the cost is sometimes absorbed into normal operating expenses, such as when your materials are prepared on the in-house copier. Some conferences, however, require substantial budgets for signs, handouts, folders and/or portfolios, name badges, plaques or other awards and related costs.

6. GRATUITIES are sometimes called service charges, but may mean the same. In most cases the conference site will au-

tomatically "plus-plus" you, meaning an automatic surcharge for gratuity, which in turn is then taxed. This is no small item and should not be overlooked as it can add more than 25 percent to your total bill. Most meeting planners have little success in negotiating these charges, so you would probably benefit more by paying them and concentrating your negotiations on the items onto which they are tacked; 25 percent of $14 is less than 25 percent of $18. In addition, there are cases where you either want to, or are *expected* to, tip beyond the already levied levels mentioned above.

7. TAXES already mentioned above, can also affect sleeping room charges. It is becoming quite common to see taxes on rooms exceed 10 percent, primarily because this is seen as taxing a group that cannot "fight back". Convention and visitors bureaus are beginning to realize the negative impact such high taxes can have on revenue, but by and large room taxes are seen as easy money for cities. If you have neglected to budget for 10 percent tax on 300 sleeping rooms at $75, you have an automatic deficit of $4,500 for a two-day meeting!

8. RECREATIONAL FEES. Are you having a golf tournament? Will you hire a bus and tour guide for a spouse trip around the area? Are you having a band or other entertainment at your banquet? All of these extras entail expenses and must be accounted for in planning the event.

9. SHIPPING. Once your materials are produced, how do you get them to the conference site? Usually by postal service, or UPS or some air freight company, but never for free. Also there are postage fees for announcement letters, confirmation letters and such. Telephone charges should also be estimated. Sometimes these two are put together under communication. (Fax charges should go here too.)

10. SPEAKER FEES AND EXPENSES can once again go from

A to Z, depending on your needs and your abilities to pay. Do you have to have a nationally known speaker? If so, it's going to cost you, probably upwards of $5,000. Can you con the local mayor into greeting you? Good. He or she usually comes free (may cost you a cup of coffee). Speaker cost can be controlled through careful consideration, again, of the real objective or goal of the meeting. Because last year's event had a dynamite speaker does not mean you have to top that. The speakers, and the fees they command, should be related to the meeting's objectives.

11. MISCELLANEOUS CHARGES. There will always be some category of expense for your meeting that does not easily fit into any of the major items listed above. It may be a fee for temporary help at your registration table, or a rented wheel-chair for the guy who broke his leg the first day of the meeting, or unplanned charges for duplication on-site (at a cost of 25 cents a copy!), or any number of other things. Just remember the adage that when it comes to meetings, Murphy was an optimist. You need a fund for contingencies.

12. FREEBIES. This one is sometimes totally missed. How many VIPs (including spouses and speakers) do you have coming for whom you have agreed to provide both room and board? Sometimes the past president, or the speakers, or at least some of them, or others for various reasons, contribute to your costs but not to your revenue. Don't forget these costs when you try to figure out the total cost of the meeting.

SELF-SUPPORTING

Let's switch now to the meeting that pays its own way or makes money. Basically the procedure for figuring the costs is the same. There might be a few extra items to consider, such as flyers and other advertising, but the categories remain the same. The difference comes in trying to figure out how to pay for it. Do you want to cover all costs through registration fees, or will you subsidize participant fees through fees charged to exhibitors? Can you get one or more events sponsored by a group who, for various reasons, would be willing to do so? For example, if your group uses computers in their work (who doesn't), perhaps either hardware or software vendors would be interested in hosting a cocktail party. Or if the group represents potential business for the host hotel in the future, perhaps the hotel would sponsor a breakfast or other function. Will you allow partial participation, or will all participants pay the full fee even if they will be there only part-time?

How about categories of registration? The possibilities are numerous, including early and late fees, member and non-member fees, different fees for different categories of membership, guest fees, and so on. Unfortunately, these decisions often are based on inter-related factors. For example, if you raise exhibitor fees you may lose exhibitors, thus you will need higher registration fees. If partial fees are not somewhat higher per unit than full fees, you will lose attendance at some functions.

The key to costing out and paying for an event lies in keeping good records of past events. What did you charge for what last year, and how many attended? Which events were "losers" and why? How should you redesign your conference to maximize the income and minimize the outflow?

In my opinion, budgeting requires careful coordination among all aspects of the conference so surprises don't knock the books out of balance. The banquet committee, if separate from the budget committee, must know limits and be expected to live within them. The budget committee must solicit input from all segments before committing to a budget and setting fees. The process should be carefully monitored as the event approaches so that, for example, telephone calls can be made to exhibitors to boost lagging sign-ups, or to solicit more sponsors for more events.

Perhaps budgeting can be best illustrated by developing a couple of examples. Let us do a budget first for a series of meetings that are not self-supporting, then one for a meeting where your job is to cover all expenses with a combination of registration fees and exhibit space rentals.

First the non-revenue meetings. Let's assume that you will be having ten training sessions during the year, each of three days' duration. The average attendance will be 25 and all will be travelling out of town to attend the sessions. On average, your hotel sleeping rooms will cost $100 per night, and your conference room rental will average $150 per day. You will have one dinner at each training session, at a cost of $40 per person, and coffee breaks will average $10 per day per person. Other meals will be paid by trainees, to be reimbursed by your firm. Assume this reimbursement will cost an average of $50 per day, $30 for the day when you furnish the dinner. Ground transportation to and from the airports at either end will cost you a total of $40 per participant. Air transportation will cost you an average of $400 per person, and miscellaneous personal expenses will average $10 per day per person. Audio-visual equipment needs will cost you $75 per day. And finally, each training session will be taught by two instructors who will receive the same reimbursement for expenses as the trainees. For the sake of this example, we will not figure salary costs, cost for developing or shipping materials, or any of the other possibilities mentioned above. Also, to simplify the mathematics, we will assume all costs listed include taxes. But again, don't you do this, because taxes can kill you if you ignore them. What will your budget need to be?

By cost item, the figures are:

Sleeping rooms (4 nights per attendee, assuming normal travel patterns) 4 × 27 × 10	1080 nights @ 100 = 108,000
Conference room rent	30 days @ $150 = $4,500
Audio-visual rent	30 days @ 75 = 2,250
Dinner 27 × 10	270 @ 40 = 10,800
Other meals $50 × 3, plus $30	270 @ 180 = 48,600
Miscellaneous 27 × 4 × 10	1080 days @ 10 = 10,800
Ground transportation 27 × 10	270 @ 40 = 10,800
Air transportation 27 × 10	270 @ 400 = 108,000
TOTAL BUDGET NEEDED	$303,750

And that's only for ten relatively small and short training sessions! The trainers better do it right!

But now let's look at a meeting where you need to make revenue cover cost. In this case, of course, you need to make some assumptions because you will be making some decisions (what price to charge) without perfect knowledge of the numbers. Here are the facts:

1. Target registration fees are $150 for participants, $90 for guests.

2. Anticipated number of participants is 500, with 200 guests.

3. You will furnish one cocktail reception and dinner, at a cost of $60 per person. Full participation is expected for this event.

4. You will furnish two refreshment breaks each day for three days at a cost of $8 per person per break. Average attendance at each break is expected to be 400.

5. You will furnish free lodging and meals for each of ten VIPs for the full four days of the conference (including a pre-conference arrival day). This will cost you $5,000.

6. Audio-visual costs for the entire conference will be $4,000.

7. Speaker fees will be $5,000.

8. Salaries for registration help, and other hired assistance will be $2,500.

9. Yours is a volunteer association, so no other salary costs need to be considered.

10. All air and ground transportation costs will be borne by participants. These costs for your VIP group will total $7,500.

11. Costs for development, printing and shipping of conference materials will total $3,000.

12. Mailing costs for solicitation flyers to potential participants will be $4,000.

13. Two continental breakfasts will be sponsored by organizations interested in your members' business. All other meals will be at the expense of participants.

14. Conference room fees will total $3,000. Exhibit hall rental is complimentary, but a setup fee of $50 per booth will be paid by you.

15. It is believed you can sell 250 booths to exhibitors. (More would be possible, but this is provided for your "break-even" point.)

16. All fees paid to the host property for items 3,4 and 6 will be subject to a "plus plus" charge (meaning tax and gratuity) of 25 percent. Items 6 and 14 are subject to an 8 percent sales tax, but no gratuity. Item 5 is subject to a 12 percent room tax.

The question is, how much will you need to charge per booth to cover all costs of the conference?

First we'll look at costs:

Reception and dinner for 700 @ $60 (+25%)	$52,500
Refreshment breaks @ $8 for 400 × 3 × 2 (+25%)	24,000
VIP rooms $5,000 + 12%	5,600
Audio-visual rent $4,000 + 8%	4,320
Speakers' fees	5,000
Salaries	2,500
Air fare etc. for VIPs	7,500
Materials	3,000
Mailing and flyers	4,000
Conference room rent $3,000 + 8%	3,240
Exhibit setup $50 × 250 + 8%	13,500
TOTAL ANTICIPATED COSTS	$125,160

Your anticipated revenues are much easier to figure:

500 participants @ $150	$75,000
200 guests @ $90	18,000
TOTAL ANTICIPATED REVENUE	$93,000
COSTS	$125,160
LESS REVENUE	93,000
NEEDED FROM BOOTHS	$32,160

If you divide $32,160 by 250, you find you will need to charge an average of $128.64 per booth. Let's assume this is too low. (And it is a *very* low figure for booth rental.) What are your options? You can lower the registration fee, raise the level of expenditures on events, (perhaps host two receptions, or a golf tournament), increase expenditures for speakers, or—make a profit. Also, don't forget the unanticipated expenses, so even if you don't want to do any of the things suggested here, you should of course raise the booth fees to a nice round figure, such as $150, to allow for these unseen but predictable contingencies.

See, I told you meeting planning was fun!

Site Selection

▶ Selecting an appropriate site for your meeting or conference is a multi-faceted task, involving costing, analyzing your participants' desires and needs, understanding the strengths and weaknesses of alternative types of properties and locations, and a variety of other factors that can affect the meeting either positively or negatively.

The first step is to analyze the needs and desires of your participants. There is no one best site for all groups. Senior managers may demand more amenities and luxury than more junior staff; the latter may want more recreational facilities than the former. Whether spouses will attend, whether participants will have cars or will be "on foot", the time of year and anticipated weather, safety factors, availability of restaurants, shopping, public transportation, distance from the airport, and ease of getting there; all these need to be considered.

One thing you should not do is to choose a site based on your own personal preference. It may be that you will not even attend the function, so your tastes are not relevant. You must choose a facility that will satisfy both the participants and the agenda. (If your group needs to meet all day every day during the winter, stay away from a golf resort, because they won't be able to use it.)

Once you have analyzed the group, it's time to begin shopping. I believe the site inspections should be done after you have an indication of which properties can or will accommodate your group within your budget. I attempt to do this by using the telephone, giving full meeting specifications and asking for a preliminary rate quote. This can be done directly with individual hotels or conference sites if you know them, or by using two invaluable sources; convention and visitors bureaus and national sales offices of chains or affiliates. If I don't know the area where I am thinking of putting a meeting, my first stop is one of these two sources, or both. Not only can they give me good advice, but they know me and my meeting needs because of past contacts, so they can pre-sell the value of my meeting to the properties they represent. Once I determine who is interested, I then ask for conference planners' brochures so I can do my homework and perhaps eliminate a few sites by looking at their pictures or analyzing their meeting room specifications. If possible, you should also obtain a map of the general area so you can both determine whether a property is downtown or suburban and plan your site inspection visits to be most efficient in terms of travel time.

A frequent mistake is trying to cram too many site visits into one day. If you look at more than five relatively large properties in a day, you probably are either not doing as thorough a job of inspection as you should be doing, or you're going to end up at the end of the day not remembering which hotel had which ballroom or boardroom. It is crucial to use some form of checklist or other note-taking guide so you remember at the conclusion of your visits what was special (either good or bad) about each property visited. A form I developed over the years in my shopping is included here as Appendix 1. I neither advocate nor denigrate the form. It serves my purpose. But you may need to develop your own form to satisfy your own special needs. If you would like, please feel free to copy my form for your own use or to modify it as you wish to serve your own needs. Whatever you do, leave time in between appointments to make notes immediately on your checklist, not after you have finished a number of visits.

Let's look at each item on my form, in order:

1. GENERAL. This section contains identifying information, including sales contacts at two levels. The reason for obtaining the two levels of contacts is that occasionally you will need to "go over" the head of the sales person in order to find someone with the authority to commit to your needed rate or other special requests. Also, personnel turnover rates are high in hotels, so two contacts are better than one.

Keep a folder on each hotel and include a conference planner's guide, if you can get one. I don't mean a rack brochure or other slick sales piece that features bikinis by poolside, but a booklet with meeting room specifications and actual pictures of the facility, as opposed to artist renderings, etc. You can save yourself a whole lot of note-taking by getting a good conference planner's guide. Note whether the site is unionized. It may or may not make a difference to your meeting, but it's nice to know, in case. Also, find out what sales affiliations the site is connected to so you can check with "your sources" in the industry to find out any additional tidbits you may not be told during your visit, such as planned renovations, or financial difficulties that the site may be suffering.

2. LOBBY. Space is provided here for your comments on the general appearance of the lobby. This will be the first point of view for your participants and, other than the sleeping room and meeting room, the space most often utilized by the group. What does it convey to you? Is it airy and friendly, gargantuan, too small and closed in, beautiful? Does it put you in a good or bad mood?

3. FRONT DESK. This is the most important contact (sometimes the only one) with the hotel staff for most of your participants. Some hotels recognize this and spend appropriate time and effort training their front desk staff to deal with customers in a polite and efficient manner. Others, unfortunately, do not. This should be observed before you make your presence known to the sales representative. After you have been identified as a meeting planner you will be afforded special treatment. Your group members will not. You need to know how they will be received. Spend a few minutes in quiet observation of procedures being followed at the front desk. Also remember to ask the salesperson about check in and check out times, as these may need to be modified for your group to accommodate your meeting hours.

4. ELEVATORS. How many elevators are there, and how good are they? Are they responsive to calls or do you have to suffer long waits before you can get on? The relative number of elevators to rooms depends in part on the number of floors. You need fewer elevators per room in a three-floor hotel than you do in a 20-story high-rise. Are the elevators easily visible from the lobby? Do they have loud bells that will interfere with the sleep of guests near the elevator?

5. SLEEPING ROOMS. Obviously a major factor in any hotel inspection is the sleeping room. Be sure that you are shown all types of rooms, or at least all types into which your group will

be put. Be wary of the "model room" that is near the sales office. This may mean that major portions of the hotel are under renovation (or worse yet, should be). What sometimes happens is that you are shown the deluxe rooms, but your rate qualifies you for the standard (lower quality) room. If the sales person cannot answer how many rooms of which type are in the hotel, do not accept this. Someone in the sales office will know, and you need to know.

My form specifies several subsections on which to make notes. You may wish to have fewer or more and almost certainly will want to have at least some which are different from the ones I use. The item labeled "Rates quoted" is of course subject to all sorts of variations, including seasonal, market, etc. It is important, of course, and should be considered not as a fixed price but as a relative price, compared to other hotels inspected at the same time. As mentioned earlier, do not forget to find out the tax rate, it can kill you!

Both the number and type of non-smoking rooms provided are important. If the hotel is vague on this item, it may mean they will designate any room as non-smoking on request. This is, of course, useless as it takes a major effort to rid a room of smoking odors after use by even a moderate smoker. Even in those cases where rooms are designated as permanently non-smoking, if they are on the same floors with smoking rooms they will be less smoke-free than if they were on special floors (or wings) that are totally smoke-free.

The item "number committable" refers to the number of rooms that can be committed to meetings. This varies depending on the type of business the site is attempting to attract. If there are 500 rooms in the hotel, but only 200 are committable for meetings, you are looking at a property with a heavy transient trade, so the hotel would want to reserve 300 rooms for this type of business. This is not necessarily a negative factor for your planning purposes. It means, for example, that meeting rooms will be more likely available to you than if 400 rooms are for meeting-related people. I mention it only because you cannot assume from the number of rooms in the hotel that your group will fit.

In looking at rooms, it is, of course, impossible not to be influenced by your own tastes and preferences, but try to remember that you are choosing for others. The fact that I have very little hair means I will not be impressed by the presence of hair dryers in the bathroom, but if the majority of my attendees don't share my condition they may find this a nice amenity. Wall colors and carpets should be viewed both for pleasant surroundings and as a gauge of how long it's been since the rooms have been renovated. Shag carpets, for example, were once popular in hotel rooms but have been "out" for years. Remote control for TV, speakers in the bathroom, telephone placement, number and type of chairs in the rooms, basic size of the room, whether there is a mini-bar, even the type of glasses provided, can all affect the acceptability of the room. I have found the minute I assume that *all* hotels now provide X, that is the time I will hit one that doesn't. I have two pet "needs" in a hotel room: AM-FM radio, and glass glasses (I hate plastic glasses). What are your pet peeves, or those which are especially important to your group?

Take your time inspecting rooms; be sure to look in the bathroom. Take notice of the level and number of lighting fixtures, notice whether the closet has a door, whether there is adequate drawer space in the dresser, check for smoke alarms and sprinklers, notice the quality of towels, the "amenities" (soap, shampoo, etc.) provided, what services are available, such as a newspaper, coffee maker, room service (what hours?), whether in-room movies or cable television is available, and at what price.

While not technically part of the room, one section on my form in the "sleeping rooms" section deals with location and price of ice and soft drinks from vending machines (Yes, Virginia, some hotels *do* charge for ice.) It doesn't sound like a big deal, but do you want to go up or down a floor for ice or a soft drink? In addition to the inconvenience, it means twice as many people will be using that machine, which doubles the chances that it will be empty or malfunctioning.

What about the view? Are your rooms ocean front or do they face the parking lot? Do guests have to be above a certain floor in order to see anything other than another building? If the views are different, are the rates different? If not, can you specify view rooms in your contract? If they are different, you better be sure to specify the type and location of the rooms you expect.

6. SUITES. Depending on your group, you may want to ignore this category entirely. It might be that you will not use a suite, so you don't care. I always try to look at suites, regardless of whether I need one for the particular meeting I'm concerned about now, for two reasons: (1) I may need to plan another meeting here soon that will require a suite; (2) I may be able to get one free, even if I don't "need" it. Depending on the ratio of suites to total rooms in the hotel, suites are sometimes quite easy to negotiate. I was once told that suites are the last rooms sold so therefore are the ones most easily "given away". Why not be a hero if you can?

If you are looking at suites, much of what I said about rooms applies here as well, plus you need to have in mind the function(s) to which the suite will be put. Will it be used for an informal evening gathering place, a private spot for one-on-one discussions, for a press conference, as a major hospitality suite, or all the above?

Again, there are often several types and categories of suites, and you need to be aware of all of them. If you want to use the suite as a gathering spot, it better not be located on a floor to which access is only by special key (often true on so called "concierge level" floors). If it will be used for business discussions, it better not have a jacuzzi in the living room. If it will be a major hospitality room it needs to be large enough for the group as opposed to a smaller but more elegant VIP suite.

7. CONCIERGE LEVEL, VIP TOWER, ETC. These words are used interchangeably to describe what is becoming a more popular concept, especially in the better hotels, one that expands, at less cost, the idea of special treatment for VIPs. It's less expensive to provide one lounge area, including cocktails and/or breakfast, than it is to build several extra suites or deluxe rooms. While there are variations, what is often involved is a separate area of the hotel, set aside for special guest treatment. Often this is a separate floor, accessible only by a special key inserted into the elevator, which allows the key-holder into a lounge where snacks, afternoon cocktails and morning continental (or full) breakfasts are provided along with a higher-priced sleeping room. This is nice, if it doesn't create protocol headaches for you. If not all of your group can be accommodated in this manner, who chooses the "lucky ones" and on what basis? If someone on the concierge level wishes to bring a colleague to the lounge as a guest, what are the procedures? If the "boss" needs to have several private conferences, then he or she would probably not want to be on the keyed concierge level, but what can you do to provide the boss with the amenities of the concierge level while residing in a suite on a different level? (One way, of course, is to negotiate for a special key for this purpose, which would allow the boss access to the special lounge even though his or her sleeping room is not on that level.)

At any rate, whether or not you intend to use the concierge

level, you should know if the hotel has it and the rules under which it operates. If your room count exceeds your block, you may find, as I did once, that the hotel has no choice other than to put part of the group on the concierge level. You will be asked to choose which of your group should be given this treatment.

8. CONFERENCE ROOMS. At last we get to the *real* reason to do a site inspection. Why have I left this until so late into the list? Of course the quality, size, location and other factors that go into a meeting room are crucial to your meeting, but I submit that the whole ambiance of the total property is also crucial. You will spend probably less than one-third of the time at the conference actually in the meeting room and the other two-thirds either in the rest of the hotel or surrounding community.

Nonetheless, you do need to pay close attention to the meeting rooms in the property. If you can help it, do not look only at the room you think you will occupy for your one meeting. Often, for many, sometimes mysterious, reasons, you will be asked to move from that room to another, or even others. Also, rooms inspected now will probably not change for at least a year or two, so this inspection can serve future as well as current meetings.

If possible obtain all materials you can regarding specifications of the meeting room *before* you take the tour. This way you can use the map and specifications to help orient yourself as you go and to make notes on aspects of the rooms that do not coincide with the specification sheets. One of the most common problems with specification sheets, and potentially the most troublesome, is the existence of pillars. If you plan a setup for a room that you expect to be free of pillars, only to find you need to work around three or four, you are in trouble. Another irritant is the misleading practice of some hotels to express their square footage to include bathrooms or alcoves that are essentially useless except for coffee breaks. As an example, here are two room drawings, each described as having the same amount of square feet. Which one would you want to use?

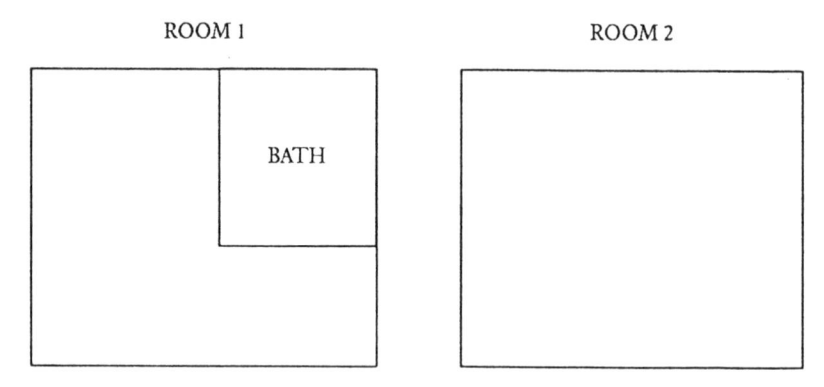

ROOM 1   ROOM 2

BATH

While touring the conference rooms, be aware of where the light controls are. It's awkward on entering a dark conference room to find the light controls are at the front of the room, and the salesperson has to grope through the dark to find them. It would be better to have light controls at both the front and back of the room, but if they can be in only one spot, they are better placed at the front so the meeting conductor can control them more easily. Note the type of lights and how much control you will have. Incandescent lights create more heat than fluorescent but provide better color clarity. Fluorescent lights often do not have variable levels; they are either on or off. This makes it impossible to dim the lights. You are forced to turn off some, leaving you with uneven light levels within the room. The best combination is one that gives you both incandescent and fluorescent lighting. Also, be aware of chandeliers. Despite their beauty, they can have two drawbacks. First, they can interfere with projection of slides or movies, and secondly, if they are exceptionally large, they can make some people nervous about sitting under them.

Chandeliers can distract attendees, but there are far more serious distractions to be concerned about. Windows, mirrors, poor sound insulation between rooms and between the room and the service corridor, type and design of floor covering, even the basic color of the room can either help or hinder your meeting. I once turned down a hotel because each of its meeting rooms had one wall which was painted a rather vivid shade of red-orange. Red is supposed to be an anger-producing color, and I didn't want to have to bring a lion tamer to the meeting.

One thing I have found almost universally true, unfortunately, is that I cannot trust the hotel's judgment on room capacities. I have developed my own rule of thumb for small meetings, which is that I need 25 square feet per person, twice as much as what some hotels say I need. There are specific reasons why my meetings need the space they do, but that is not the point I wish to make. My point is that you need to determine, through experience, how much space you need, on the average, for your meetings. Obviously requirements vary depending on whether you need a conference, theater, classroom, hollow square, or other set-up, so you may need to have several rules and insist on sticking to them. (Some of the more common types of room setups are illustrated here. You can see for yourself, why I say that requirements vary.)

Remember that hotels make most of their profit through the sale of sleeping rooms, so they want to keep the larger meeting rooms available for the groups that use the most bedrooms. They don't want to have to turn away a group because you are using the ballroom but only 25 sleeping rooms. If you need an inordinate amount of meeting space, you may have to pay extra for it, but if you need it, you need it. Be sure you get it.

The location of the meeting room is also important. Is it convenient to restrooms? Can coffee breaks be served easily without disturbing the meeting? What about traffic flow? Will

CONFERENCE STYLE

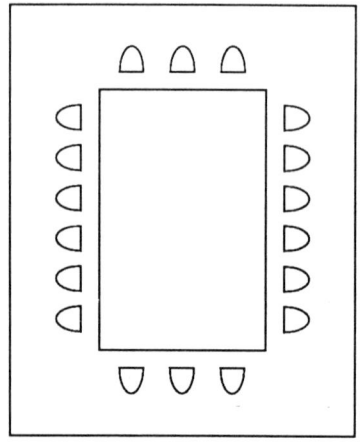

THEATER STYLE

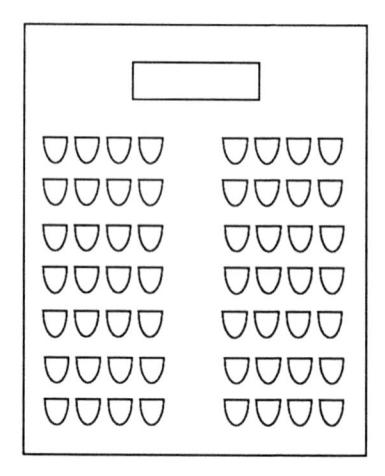

CLASSROOM STYLE

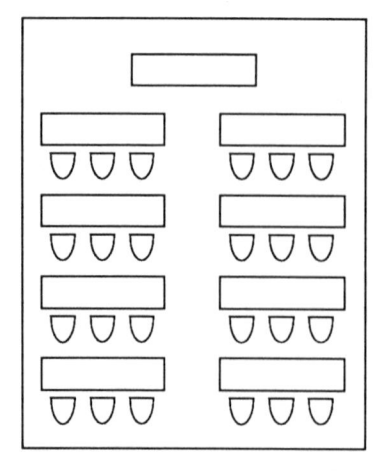

U-SHAPED

you be hearing several other groups either in transit past your room or in breaks outside your room? If you are isolated, are you so isolated that your participants will have trouble finding the place? If you are using several rooms, are they in proximity so you can share coffee breaks, or will you need separate breaks?

FIVE FOOT ROUNDS

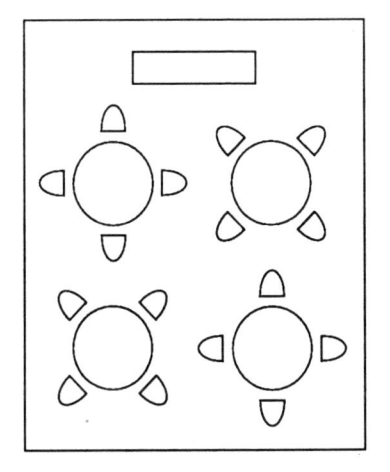

SIX FOOT ROUNDS

CHEVRON STYLE

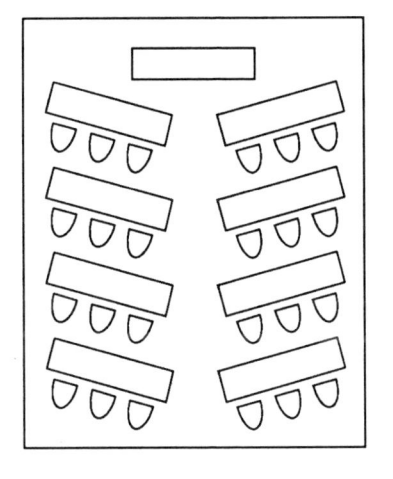

RECEPTION STYLE

(NO SEATING REQUIRED)

Is the transition between rooms easy or difficult? How far are you from the restaurants or other facilities of the hotel? Does your room overlook the pool so you will hear children at play during the meeting?

The walls in the meeting room are also important. To provide flexibility, hotels often use portable walls, (air walls, folding solid walls, or even, in some less expensive hotels, accordion walls) between meeting rooms. The best wall for sound insulation is a solid wall. Next best is a setup using air walls with a dead space between meeting rooms (a corridor, with another air wall between you and the adjacent meeting room). Next in terms of desirability is the air wall with no space between rooms, then the folding solid wall, and at the very bottom of the list is the accordion wall. I will not use the latter unless I absolutely have to.

Temperature controls in a meeting room can be a real problem. If you have to call the engineer to change the temperature setting you may have to wait at least several minutes before your room begins to adjust to your needs. On the other hand, if you can control the setting yourself, so can everyone else in the room; and believe me, you will *never* have everyone comfortable at the same time. The best you can do is to try to hit a happy medium. My preference is to have the room settings controlled by a responsive engineering staff. This means two things to the meeting planner. First, I have to be in the room before the meeting starts so I can check the temperature and have it adjusted if necessary. Remember, before people arrive the room should be a little too cool because each person acts as a miniature heater, giving off 98-degree temperatures. Secondly, if you are the speaker the room will seem warmer to you than to others, for two reasons: (1) you are active and standing up, and (2) if you're a good speaker you have some nervous energy going for you, which will warm you up more.

9. REFRESHMENT BREAK SERVICE. I also check my list as to type of coffee and other break service provided. It seems a minor point because one would think that all hotels serve coffee in china or some equivalent service, and that the prices are nearly

the same. As to price, *not so*! Price variations are surprising, even within the same city and can even double between two otherwise seemingly comparable hotels. As to china service, the first time you are surprised by foam cups you will understand the necessity of checking this out beforehand. Also important are such things as the equipment used to keep coffee warm. Is it a container with a burner underneath or merely an insulated carafe? Is decaffinated coffee brewed or packaged instant?

Notice that my checklist does not provide space for discussing meal service and process. That is because most of my meetings do not require meal service. There are, however, many details here too that need to be examined and listed if you need meal service at your meeting. Some of these needs can be satisfied by obtaining and attaching a catering menu, but many cannot. How many people does the hotel expect each waiter to serve? How many will be seated at each table? Will the staff adjust menus to suit your needs, or are they interested only in serving fixed meals on the menu?

10. AUDIO-VISUAL POLICIES. What does the hotel provide without charge? What are the charges for equipment you need to rent, and will they give you trouble if you want to use other than the "in-house" supplier? I have saved as much as 40 percent by shopping around for this service. "Let your fingers do the walking" a little bit, or call the local Convention and Visitors Bureau for references if you prefer. As with most other things, these items are sometimes negotiable as well.

11. RESTAURANTS. The importance of this section of the checklist increases with the isolation of the hotel from other opportunities for meals and relaxation. If the hotel is in the middle of a downtown area where you can walk to 25 other restaurants, this section is not crucial. However, the breakfast hours, service and process will always be important because most

people don't want to travel far for breakfast. Breakfast hours are important in order to avoid a crush just before your meeting begins. Even if you have three hours of service before your meeting starts, remember that you may still have a rush 30 minutes beforehand. Everyone assumes there will be room for him(her) just before meeting time. If your group is large and the dining room small, you may find that buffet service, either for breakfast or lunch, can be a real lifesaver.

If the hotel you are considering is somewhat isolated, of course this section of the checklist takes on added importance. Again, consideration of your participants' budgets must be a part of your thinking. I have turned down beautiful hotels with sleeping-room rates within our budget because the prices in their restaurants, or their dress codes, would have been unpopular with our participants.

12. BARS/LOUNGES. After your group has been all day in meeting, what types of facilities are there to encourage, or at least permit, the informal networking that can be so important to the success of your conference? Is there a happy hour or some other type of enticement for the group to assemble and talk informally? What time does the band start, if there is one, and will its volume drive your people out or preclude discussion below a shout? Are there optional gathering spots, not necessarily bars, but lobby areas, game room or the like? Also, don't forget to check prices in these outlets as well. And if you are planning a group cocktail reception, make sure that the hotel's public happy hour is not a better deal than yours. If it is, consider asking for a section of the lounge to be set aside for your group as opposed to having your own party.

13. RECREATIONAL FACILITIES. Other than the bars/lounges above, what can your group do to unwind from the rigors of listening to speeches all day? As our society becomes

more health conscious, recreational facilities are becoming more important to meeting planners. Not just the existence of such facilities but their usability, both in terms of hours and cost, are important. I once had a major problem because for some inexplicable reason the exercise room closed each day at 5:00 P.M., exactly when our sessions ended. Apparently the working hours of the room attendant were more important to the hotel management than the wishes of its paying guests. Such seemingly minor factors as how you get to the facility may have a negative impact on the enjoyment your group gets from the site and therefore their attitude toward the conference. For example, do they have to parade across the lobby in their swimsuits to get to the swimming pool, or are there back elevators or changing rooms that allow them more privacy? Is the jogging course on or off-site? If off-site, is it safe? Is there a charge for any activities? If so, what?

14. TRANSPORTATION. Because most of my meetings are held downtown, about the only transportation costs I am interested in are those incurred getting to and from the airport, so that's what my checklist covers. But if your group will need to go to restaurants, find out if cabs are convenient and affordable. If there is a hotel van, is it available only during certain hours or all the time? Can it be "reserved" exclusively for your group? At what cost or obligation? Does it do pickup as well as delivery, or is the return trip from the restaurant or shopping center "on your own"? Does it have a limited radius of operation? What is it?

15. PARKING. This is, of course, self explanatory, except that you need to find out whether the parking facility is owned by the hotel or is a franchised operation. If hotel-owned, the chances of negotiating rates are usually better. What are the rates for "locals" (participants who are not staying at the hotel)?

16. STAFF ATTITUDE. This is perhaps one of the most critical aspects of a successful conference site and yet one of the most difficult to measure. For one thing, you probably won't see much of the conference staff when you do a site inspection; you will typically be with a salesperson who won't be around during the meeting. You can't ask, "How's your staff attitude?" If you do, you'll be told that they have all been there for years and love the place. I look for little things. I have already covered observing the front desk staff. How about the housekeeping staff? Do they know the salesperson or are they treated like strangers? Are they efficient and apparently organized, or are there piles of laundry and towels in several places in the corridors? What about the ashtrays near the elevators, are they clean or full? Same for the lobby, is it neat or in disarray? If the salesperson sees a piece of paper on the floor, does he or she pick it up? If you happen to notice a cracked glass or a burned-out light bulb in a room, does he or she call it in immediately, make a note to call later, or ignore it? These are the little things that can irritate or please your group during their stay.

17. LOCATION OF FACILITY. Where is it? The importance of this topic has been discussed above but it is important to note, especially when you are examining several properties on one day or one trip.

18. OTHER COMMENTS. This is sometimes the most important part of the form. Here is where you put comments made in passing by the salesperson or others during your site inspection. Maybe it will be the best restaurant in town, or the fact that a major renovation is about to begin and won't end until just after your meeting. It's also a convenient place to jot notes during your walk, which can later be transferred to the form in the proper location. Maybe you want to say which suite the VIP should get or note that the salesperson will be quitting next week,

so any deals made need to be recorded quickly and on paper. Whatever you need to say that isn't covered by the form in an explicit manner can be entered here.

I sometimes use this section of the form to record an informal ranking of the several properties I have examined that day. While it seems like all the detail already recorded should do that for you, confusion may set in as to the relative weights to assign to a better meeting room as opposed to a less desirable location. Your overall "feel" for the place can be entered here in your own words.

APPENDIX 1

SITE INSPECTION REPORT

From MEETING MANAGEMENT
copyright Randy Talbot, 1990

1. GENERAL

Site inspection completed by _____ Date _____

_____
NAME

_____
FACILITY NAME

_____
ADDRESS

_____
CITY, STATE, ZIP

_____
TELEPHONE   FAX

Sales Contact:

_____
NAME

_____
TITLE

_____
DIRECTOR OF SALES

Conference Planners Guide Attached: ☐Yes ☐No

Union Property: ☐Yes ☐No

Affiliated with _____

2. LOBBY

Size, accommodates how many? _____

Appearance: ☐Excellent ☐Very Good
☐Fair ☐Poor

Comments _____
_____
_____

Bell Desk: ☐Yes ☐No

Facilities for luggage storage _____

3. FRONT DESK

Check in time _____ Check out _____

Computerized check in/out: ☐Yes ☐No

Number of staff on duty during peak hours _____

Staff Attitude _____

Rooms held without guarantee until _____

Credit cards accepted _____

4. ELEVATORS

Number _____

Easily accessible: ☐Yes ☐No

Service: ☐Excellent ☐Adequate ☐Slow

Comments _____

5. SLEEPING ROOMS

Total number ____	Double/Double ____	Accessible rooms ____
King ____	Double ____	Non-smoking ____
Queen ____	Twin ____	Number committable ____

Rates quoted: Single _____ Double _____ Tax rate _____

Appearance: ☐Excellent ☐Very Good ☐Adequate ☐Poor

Fire Safety: ☐Smoke alarms ☐Yes ☐No Sprinklers ☐Yes ☐No

Amenities—Standard (e.g. shampoo, showercap): ☐Yes ☐No

Others—list (e.g. coffee, newspaper, HBO) _____

Comments _____

Room service: ☐Yes ☐No Hours _____

Vending machines   Location   Cost

   Soda machine   _____   _____

   Ice machine   _____   _____

   Other   _____   _____

6. SUITES

Floor plan(s) attached: ☐Yes ☐No

Total number available _____

Policy re complimentary suites _____

Type	Number	Capacity	Rate	Facilities
____	_____	_____	____	_____
____	_____	_____	____	_____
____	_____	_____	____	_____

Appearance: ☐Excellent ☐Very good
           ☐Fair ☐Poor

Comments _____
_____
_____

7. CONCIERGE LEVEL, VIP TOWER, ETC. ☐Yes ☐No

Number of floors _____

Number of rooms _____

Rates quoted: Single _____ Double _____

Extra amenities (list) _____

Complimentary services

Continental breakfast: ☐Yes ☐No

Hors d'oeuvres: ☐Yes ☐No

Liquor: ☐Yes ☐No

Other, list _____

Special keyed access: ☐Yes ☐No

Comments on VIP level _____

8. CONFERENCE ROOMS

Room specifications attached: ☐Yes ☐No

(If yes, answer all items not covered in floor plan. If no, complete all items.)

Number of meeting rooms:

                    Under 500 square feet   _____

                    500–999 square feet   _____

                    1000–1499 square feet   _____

                    1500 and over square feet   _____

                              Total   _____

Carpeted: ☐Yes ☐No

Individual controls for each room

Heat: ☐Yes ☐No   ☐Air: ☐Yes ☐No   Light: ☐Yes ☐No

Sound: ☐Yes ☐No

Obstructions: ☐Yes ☐No

If yes, describe _____

Appearance: ☐Excellent ☐Very good
            ☐Fair ☐Poor

Rest room access and size _____

Comments _____

9. REFRESHMENT BREAK SERVICE

Menu attached: ☐Yes ☐No

COST

Coffee, tea, decaf.   _____ per _____

Soft drinks   _____ per _____

Danish   _____ per _____

Juice   _____ per _____

Indicate usual service:

☐China ☐Foam ☐Other

10. AUDIO-VISUAL POLICIES

Is price list attached? ☐Yes ☐No

Which equipment is provided by property at no cost (exclude built-in equipment)

☐Podium   ☐Flip chart pads   ☐Other

☐Blackboards   ☐Screen   _____

☐Flip chart   ☐Microphone

Is A/V supplier located on site? ☐Yes ☐No

Can outside service be used? ☐Yes ☐No

Comments _____

11. RESTAURANTS

Name _____   _____   _____

Type _____   _____   _____

Price range _____   _____   _____

Meals served _____   _____   _____
   (e.g. breakfast, lunch, dinner)

Buffets served _____   _____   _____
   (indicate which meals)

No-smoking sections (yes or no)

_____   _____   _____

Seating for _____   _____   _____
Credit cards? _____   _____   _____

12. BARS AND LOUNGES

Name _____   _____   _____

Type _____   _____   _____
    (e.g. formal, casual, lobby)

Happy hour

Time _____   _____   _____

Policy _____   _____   _____

Comments _____

13. RECREATIONAL FACILITIES (Show cost, if any)

Swimming pool ☐Yes ☐No   Sauna ☐Yes ☐No

   Indoor _____ Outdoor _____   Tennis courts ☐Yes ☐No

Whirlpool ☐Yes ☐No   Jogging course ☐Yes ☐No

   Indoor _____ Outdoor _____   Other _____

Exercise room ☐Yes ☐No

Describe accessibility and policies re any off-site recreational facilities

_____

14. TRANSPORTATION (to and from airport)

Hotel limousine: Frequency   _____

               Cost   _____

Other limousine: Frequency   _____

               Cost   _____

Taxi approximate cost   _____

Hotel van available on request? ☐Yes ☐No

15. Parking

Availability _____

Cost _____

16. Staff Attitude ☐ Excellent ☐ Very good

☐ Adequate ☐ Poor

17. Location of Facility (proximity to restaurants, shopping, public transportation, entertainment facilities, etc.)

_____
_____
_____

18. Other Comments _____

_____
_____
_____
_____
_____
_____
_____
_____
_____
_____
_____
_____
_____
_____
_____
_____

8

Exhibits

✏️ At many conferences or trade shows, as they are also called, there are exhibits for participants to visit, usually for the purpose of shopping for products or services displayed in the exhibit booths. As the meeting manager, your job is to satisfy two basic goals: (1) You must make the expenditure for the booth worthwhile for the exhibitors in terms of business generated for them; (2) You must make enough money for your organization from the booth rentals to substantially reduce your total expenses of the conference. (In some cases, you are asked to make more than that required to cover expenses, perhaps to make a profit to pay for your salary or other items.) It requires careful balancing of several points to achieve a happy medium. Among the items to consider, which we will discuss separately here, are the following: size of booths, number of booths, price(s) for the booths, times of day and number of hours for the exhibit, enticements to generate booth traffic, possible conflicts with exhibit plans, types of booth design, rules and regulations for exhibits, number of people allowed in each booth, controlling traffic in the exhibit area, electrical or other special needs, setup and breakdown time, freight drayage and storage, and security. Solve all these puzzles to everyone's satisfaction and you're a hero; fall down on a few and you could find yourself in deep trouble, especially for future events. Before getting into the specifics listed here, however, let's address some overall questions which may occur to the first-time exhibit planner.

WHERE TO BEGIN

Whom should you contact to begin discussions on exhibits? If the exhibits will be in the hotel with the rest of your conference, you may be working with either your primary sales contact or with the catering or convention services manager. If the exhibits will be in another location, say the local convention center, there will be an equivalent position in a sales office of the convention center where you can begin your discussions. If in the hotel, you may assume rules and policies applying to the exhibits will be the same as those applying to other functions in the hotel. There will be, however, some different questions to be answered from those you may be used to asking for your meetings. You need to know amount of weight allowed per square foot, for example. Logistical problems involved in moving freight, placement of loading docks, and the schedule for delivery of other items, such as food, to the hotel will need to be determined. Salespeople or convention managers can get these answers for you, but it may take a little time and effort on their part. If the exhibits will be in the convention center, you may be operating with a totally different set of rules. For example, different centers have different rules as to who is responsible for cleaning during the show. If you don't ask the right questions, you may end up paying twice for cleaning the carpet, once to the decorator, who routinely builds the cost into his or her bid, and once to the hall because they insist on doing it themselves. If you know whose responsibility this is you can delete the cost from one bid, but it's your job to know what charges are where.

Your first stop should once again be the convention and visitors bureau. I do not know of a directory of convention centers as such, but any convention bureau will have information on such centers or other possibilities for exhibits in the city or area. If there is only one convention center in town, how can you bargain? The answer is, you really can't if you have already agreed and signed a contract with the hotel for the rest of your function. So you need to make your wants and desires known, and find out your options before you negotiate with anybody. What about food in the convention center, for example? Some centers will allow you to choose from a selected list of caterers, some insist on only one caterer, and some will give you totally free rein.

Unions are another potential source of problems. It seems terribly short-sighted to me, but apparently there are some cities where you literally can't get anything done without running into a jurisdictional dispute between unions about whose job it is to sweep floors or hang drapes. I have heard stories about needing to have a pocket full of cash to get union members to do what you need done in a timely fashion. You need to know about this before you negotiate and avoid such cases where you can. Unfortunately, this information will not be easily gleaned from the convention bureau. You will have to check with other organizations who have used the center in the past to check on potential problem areas such as this.

When you have exhibits, you will need to use a decorator or show management firm. These people do decorations, security, storage (before, during and after the show), arrange for shipping, and a host of other activities that are specialized. I believe you should talk to them early and try to use them as extensions of your staff. It may be necessary for you to make a contingency arrangement with one firm before asking them to work with you on such details as I've laid out here. That is, if you go to this city, you will use this decorator. But once you have chosen a firm, use their expertise in dealing with exhibit vendors. That's what they do best.

Using all the information generated here and taking into account all the specific points I listed above, you then need to negotiate not separately for the exhibit space but jointly, for your conference and exhibits. When you have only one exhibit hall in town, you particularly need the extra leverage to assist you in negotiations. The leverage works both ways, of course. If you are having trouble getting a particular concession from the hotel, and the convention center salesperson knows this snag might lose exhibit hall rental for them, you might find an unexpected ally.

Let us look now at the specific points that I listed above and discuss each in turn.

SIZE OF BOOTHS

How big should each booth be? Should you have different size booths for different purposes and, if so, how many of each? The primary consideration here is the purpose of the booth, or the product or service being displayed. If you are doing booths for antiques, you need some depth to each booth to allow some room setup. The arrangement of antiques in it encourages shoppers to imagine how these antiques would look in their homes. On the other hand, if the vendors are displaying hotel brochures the space needed may not require as much depth. Likewise, the width of each booth may vary depending on the items displayed. Whatever the decision, it is important to make all booths the same size, unless there is some overriding reason to allow some booths to be bigger: for example to compensate for an awkward corner, poor lighting, or some other problem that might make a particular booth less desirable than others. Rather than granting a larger (but still undesirable) booth, it may be better to leave a gap, or to use that space for some non-vendor activity such as newsletter distribution, committee sign-ups or some other purpose. Don't forget that vendors who want to have an unusual display can rent more than one booth adjacent to each other. If your show is mixed in terms of booth types, for example some food booths mixed in with antiques, there may be a need to have different sizes for different functions. You may also develop other problems with mixed booths, by the way, like the time my wife's booth of lace pillows was placed just downwind from the cotton candy booth.

NUMBER OF BOOTHS

The number of booths you should have depends on three primary items: the size of the space available, the number you think you can sell, and the traffic you expect to be able to generate for each booth. The first item, size of space, may seem trivial in that you can make that decision based on the other two. However, if you don't really know how many you can sell and you rent a space which is too large for your function, you not only pay more than you should, you also limit the number of properties you can consider for your event and end up with an embarrassingly empty exhibit hall. For example, if you decide you will need 20,000 square feet of exhibit space, many hotels will be unable to accommodate your event, thus limiting your options for negotiation. If you later find your booths occupy only half that space, you might incur extra expense draping off the unused portion of the exhibit hall. Don't forget, by the way, to allow for ample aisle space in estimating your total exhibit space needs. An easy rule of thumb is to double the square footage that the actual booths take up (called net square feet). This will allow for nine to ten foot aisles and some seating. Also, when you negotiate rental prices be sure you know whether the rate quoted refers to net or gross square feet.

As to the number you think you can sell, this is, of course, based to some extent on your group's history (if there is one). How many did you sell last year? You also must consider the relative merits of this year's location versus last year's and the degree of satisfaction experienced by last year's vendors. (One excellent way to find out about vendor satisfaction is to hold a vendor caucus immediately after the trade show, getting their opinions while memories are fresh.) You may need to anticipate either growth or a drop-off, depending on these two points (i.e. your experience last year and vendor satisfaction).

Also consider carefully the amount of traffic you think you can generate for the vendors. If you have 200 booths and only 150 "shoppers", your vendors will not be happy. You might be better off to limit the number of booths to that for which you think you can generate adequate traffic. In fact, limiting the number of booths—and advertising you are doing so when you solicit exhibitors—may significantly increase the value of each booth. It may even generate as much money as renting a larger number of booths on an unlimited basis.

Related to the number of booths is the space needed for registration and for such items as an exhibit office and press facilities, or space to distribute newsletters, show new products or services available through the organization, or for authors' discussion of issues pertaining to the group's business. These functions do not require a lot of space and can sometimes be negotiated as a "freebie".

PRICE(S) OF BOOTHS

All things being equal, you should, of course, try to maximize the revenue generated from your booth rental. After all, remember that one of your two basic purposes for having booths is to cover the cost of other conference events, such as banquets. But don't lose track of the counter-balancing purpose, which is to make the booths worthwhile to the exhibitors, meaning the price paid is not out of line with the business generated. Perhaps the best gauge available here is to check prices paid by your potential vendors at other similar shows. As to one price versus varied-level pricing, that depends on both the type of booth and the exhibit hall layout. Some corner booths, for example, with double exposure to participants, may be worth more than standard booths. Booths at the entrance may be more desirable than those at the back of the hall. As mentioned earlier, you can allow double booths at double prices for those who want to make a bigger "splash".

If you have some booths that are more desirable than others to vendors, you have two marketing options to consider; either charge more for them, or sell the booths on a first-come-first-served basis, thus encouraging early sign-up in order to get the best booths. Whatever your decision, be sure that you do not change it after you begin selling unless you are prepared to go back and change the rules for all vendors, not just those you are desperately trying to enlist at the last minute. A variation on this theme you may consider is to give discounts for booth sign-ups prior to a specified date.

However you decide to price your booths, do not forget that booth rental is not all gravy. Your income must cover the direct costs generated by the exhibit, including hall rental, security, audio-visual equipment needed, decorator costs (drapes, carpet, tables), and signs.

TIMES OF DAY AND NUMBER OF HOURS

Once again we are facing a balancing act. You need enough hours to allow shoppers to visit all booths but not enough to bore the shoppers, or for the vendors to experience substantial down time when no visitors are to be seen in the aisle, let alone at the booth. Fatigue, for both vendors and shoppers, is also a factor. You may be better off with two or more relatively brief exhibit periods rather than one long one because the feet can give out before the booths do, meaning either some booths are missed, or the visitors are paying less than eager attention to what they are seeing.

Time of day is also important. This is partially dependent on what other events are going on: plan so you don't have conflicts. Seminars are generally thought to be better scheduled for the morning, for example. So you might be more or less forced into having your exhibit hours later in the day to maximize traffic. Again, you want for both the shoppers and vendors to have enough energy to survive the exhibit, so don't make the time of the exhibits too late, and don't make them too early (say Saturday morning at 8:00 A.M.). The best way to determine both time and length of exhibit hours is to listen to your participants, both shoppers and vendors. Learn from prior events, and make a serious effort to serve the needs of both groups.

ENTICEMENTS

What can you do to generate traffic for your vendors? I have seen several different techniques used, some good and some I found to be incredibly bad. One very popular device is to offer door prizes, with mandatory presence necessary for winners. This operates on the theory that shoppers will shop if they need to be there anyhow (in this case to win). Another is for vendors to give away "goodies", which come in an amazing array of forms, from candy bars to vacations. Games, such as putting contests, roulette, etc. can be used to draw traffic. There are any number of other ways to generate traffic. One word of caution, however, is that you should use something that will draw real shoppers, as opposed to someone looking merely for a prize.

Perhaps the worst example of a traffic generation scheme I have seen occurred when the planner arranged for a local high school band to march through the general session as its conclusion and to lead the shoppers to the exhibit hall. First the band was late, which made the general session drag on. Second, many people, including myself, resented the childish act of marching through the hotel to the exhibit hall as if we were back in school. Finally, after all the trouble of coming to our conference, the band wanted a chance to play for us, and they did so for at least 30 minutes! If you had paid rental fees to watch your selling hours go up in smoke while a too-loud band played march music, would you as a vendor have been happy?

Another mistake we made (I told you I learned the hard way) was to announce door or booth prizes at frequent intervals. I believe our theory was to make people stay there throughout the event, not just at the end. What we forgot was that loud-speaker announcements every 30 minutes, sometimes lasting five minutes while we located a winner, were very disruptive to communication between shopper and vendor.

The basic idea of exhibit enticements is to provide something that is of value to your shoppers but which is not so highly valued as to make them forget the real reason they are supposed to be there—to do business.

But what are some good positive enticements to increase booth traffic? Food functions are popular. Have lunch served in the exhibit hall and you will get shoppers. If you do this remember to lengthen the booth hours enough to account for the down time while individuals eat. There is an added plus possibility here because if vendors are allowed to join shoppers at lunch (eating in shifts, to keep their booths staffed) there is opportunity for additional casual conversation between buyer and seller. You could serve snacks among the booths, having servers pass food on trays. Perhaps an event newsletter can be generated, emphasizing the benefits of show attendance and making it seem like a chance not to be missed. An excellent idea used by three vendors from the same town (they happened to be hotels) involved sending out puzzle pieces that were the missing links in a picture puzzle. Only one winner was allowed per booth, but three puzzle pieces, one from each booth, were sent to each registered shopper. The traffic was terrific (as the old song goes)! Everyone wanted to see if his puzzle piece was the one. The prize was minor, something like a bottle of wine, but the contest was the thing.

Comfort is important. Exhibit halls are usually hard-floored. While carpets in the corridors help, the padding is usually thin. When the feet wear out, as I said before, the interest wanes. How about some refreshment stands, *with chairs please*, interspersed throughout the hall? Or as an individual vendor did with good success, put really thick carpeting in your booth so people come in to rest their feet. Incidentally, if you have last-minute booth cancellations, rather than have an unsightly gap in the display, fill the hole with a rest area.

How about a door prize that requires, for eligibility, the endorsement of a minimum number of vendors? A scavenger hunt might work, provided you don't let it become the primary focus of the potential shoppers. A trivia quiz, asking which booth featured the _____, door prizes posted at different points within the hall—there are many ways to make the exhibit fun as well as educational for your participants. Think creatively, and dare to try something different, always, of course, within the guidelines of keeping the focus primarily on what it is the vendors are selling.

CONFLICTS

Other than noisy distractions like the band, what are other things to watch for in planning your exhibits? I already mentioned conflicting activities, such as seminars. I feel that during booth hours no event should be scheduled to compete with booth activity. Other conflicts can come from outside your control. For example, if you have sports fans in attendance and your exhibit hours conflict with the Super Bowl, you have a major problem. Depending on your location, you may need to watch out for golf tournaments, shopping opportunities, pool time, any variety of other distracting options that may tempt your audience.

TYPES OF BOOTH DESIGN

What kinds of booths will you allow? Are you going to provide "pipe and drape," (which forms semi-private booths), eight-foot draping just for the back of the booth with three-foot halfdrapes between booths? Or maybe just table-top displays, with no large exhibits or structures allowed? Will you allow electricity in your booths? If so, make sure the hotel can meet the electrical demand. How will the cords be run? How will you control the noise if someone wants to play a videotape next to another booth where the exhibitor wants to do the same thing? If you don't allow electrical hookups, will your lighting be adequate for all vendors? How can an exhibitor demonstrate a computer without electricity? Will a phone hookup be needed to some remote computer facility or to call in sales? What you do, of course, depends on the purpose of your exhibits and the types of exhibitors. For example, if your show consists of hotels and conference sites, the larger properties may want elaborate booths while the smaller, more budget-minded properties would prefer table-top booths so they can more easily compete, at least visibly, with their neighbors. Will rigid walls be available to exhibitors? If so, can they attach anything to them, or are they "off limits"? All these decisions need to be made known to your potential exhibitors so they can plan accordingly.

My advice here is to make your initial decision, then make sure your vendors have both the opportunity and the responsibility to specify any special needs or plans in their application for booth space. In this way you can either place booths far enough apart so the two videotapes do not compete, or if necessary you can tell a vendor that his needs cannot be accommodated. Better to inform the vendor ahead of time and perhaps lose a booth rental than to wait and be taken by surprise and then have to remit the fee and make an enemy in the bargain.

RULES AND REGULATIONS

Will you, or should you, place any limitations on what your vendors can do during the show? Perhaps yes, perhaps no, depending on your shoppers and vendors. Using again the hotels as an example, you might want to limit giveaways to minor cost items so smaller properties can compete on an even basis. Or you may decide to eliminate *all* giveaways, so you make sure your shoppers are serious instead of "goodies" collectors. It is sometimes necessary to limit activities of booth occupants also. For example, at one show I saw vendors from one booth actually approaching shoppers at other booths, trying to entice them away to visit theirs. Needless to say there were many complaints.

NUMBER OF PEOPLE PER BOOTH

You are not just selling booth space for an exhibit. You are selling an opportunity to sell. And it follows that two people can sell more than one. And three (or four) can sell more than two. But at some point you need to limit the number of people who can occupy each booth. You may also want to limit the number of vendor employees who can be on the exhibit floor at any one time, or you may have two booth occupants but five other employees of that firm shopping the competition. Generally speaking the booth size should give you a good guideline as to number of occupants. They should fit comfortably within the booth so they don't interfere with traffic flow. Experienced exhibitors know what is necessary and appreciate the limits.

EXHIBIT AREA TRAFFIC

I already mentioned vendors "shopping the competition". What about non-vendors? If I haven't rented a booth, am I to be allowed on the exhibit floor? Why? Again, you are not selling space, you're selling an opportunity to sell. If I haven't paid the price, I shouldn't be given the opportunity. This means, incidentally, that you will need door watchers to keep out those who should not be in the exhibit area. Perhaps different colored badges for vendors and shoppers can be used, or tickets that need to be shown or surrendered to obtain access. A related problem I have yet to solve involves those non non-exhibiting vendors who do not enter the exhibit area but who hang around just outside it so they can accost the customers either on the way in or out (or both!). They of course have a right to be in the general area. I just hope their actions are seen by shoppers in a negative light so they don't generate business from what I consider to be unethical actions.

ELECTRICAL OR OTHER SPECIAL NEEDS

I already mentioned this above, but it's worth repeating. You need to know not only whether you will have enough outlets for your vendors but whether the capacity of the system is adequate for the demand. I once heard of a show where the hotel was not informed that many exhibitors were hair dressers who would be using hair dryers in their booths. As each hair dryer draws 1200 watts of electricity, it wasn't long before the fuses blew (both the hotel's fuses and the vendors' fuses). Other special needs should be anticipated also. Hair dressers, to continue an example, also need water. Plant displays need water. Load factors need to be considered so you don't collapse the exhibit hall under the weight of your display tractors. Sound barriers, lighting, aisle width, carpeting—all of these need to be measured in designing, pricing, selling and managing your exhibit space.

SETUP AND BREAKDOWN
How much time will be needed by your vendors to set up their displays? How about knockdown? How much will this cost you in rental fees from the exhibit hall? Decorator setup needs to occur at least one-half day prior to exhibitor setup, to allow ample time to lay down booth lines, setup pipe and drape, lay carpet, and tape down wires. If you have scheduled a conflicting conference event during the time when your vendors will be setting up displays, will they feel left out of something that is important to them?

FREIGHT, DRAYAGE AND STORAGE
When you have exhibits, you have need for major shipping and storage. In addition to the items being displayed, the booths often consist of elaborate backdrops, computers and various support devices. Convention centers and hotels often will not accept these materials before the day established as your setup day. Since you don't want to take a chance that all materials will be shipped exactly on time, you will need an interim receiving

facility and an ability to transfer goods locally from that facility to the center on setup day. Likewise, at the end of the show materials need to be repacked in crates, removed promptly from the center and stored temporarily until freight carriers can pick them up. This is one more area where your decorator or show management firm comes into play. They will receive goods, transfer them to the convention center floor, remove empty boxes once the displays are set up, and reverse the process at the end of the show. Obviously, all these services are not provided free of charge. These charges are normally paid by exhibitors separately from booth rental fees. However, since you are using only one decorator, it becomes your responsibility to make sure the fees charged are reasonable, so your vendor exhibitors are not unpleasantly surprised by outrageous storage or drayage fees.

I could tell disaster stories about shipping, drayage and storage, but you can imagine for yourself the possibilities for lost or mixed-up crates, damaged merchandise, mis-shipped items and the like. You need to check the track record of your decorator on these functions before signing up. Obviously the term "decorator" is a misnomer. They do a lot more than fix up floral displays and hang drapes!

SECURITY

Last, but certainly not least, is the matter of security. If setup is to be the day before the exhibit, someone has to make sure the exhibits are still there and intact when the show opens. This is generally available through the conference or exhibit facility but, like anything else in life, at a price. If not included in the center's rental price, security can be arranged through your decorator. Definitely don't do it yourself, use a professional. If you know your security needs, and you negotiate their costs up front, you can make sure the booth price includes the cost of security. If you forget it, you pay for it.

9

Negotiating for Facilities

▷ Now that you know what you want and what is available, how are you going to get it at a price you can afford and at a time which is optimal to your needs? There have been volumes written on the fine art of negotiating, whether it be for conference space, purchase of a car or appliance, or for how to get your way in a number of situations. What can I say in a chapter to add to these mountains of wisdom?

Perhaps, even probably, not much. So I won't even try. What I will do instead is to give you some of the basic tenets that apply specifically to negotiating for hotel or conference space, some special language, or "buzz words", and some considerations of give and take, which you must evaluate for yourself when bargaining in this industry.

First for definitions. There are a variety of terms that apply in a special manner to hotels. Words such as rack rate, corporate rate, transient rate, group rate, shoulder season, high and low season, government rate, SMURF (and other) special market rates, single, double, double-double, twin, queen and king and of course such wonderful terms as standard, special, deluxe, suite, junior suite, executive suite, hospitality suite, concierge level and others will boggle your mind if you let them. And so far we're talking only about sleeping rooms! Add to that conference room setup terms such as rounds, conference style, schoolroom, theater, hollow square, reception and banquet, to name a few, and it's hard to know where to begin.

But let's jump right in and begin by defining terms that apply to sleeping rooms:

SLEEPING ROOMS

1. RACK RATE refers to the rate you will be quoted if you call and ask for room availability. The term probably derives from the brochures you will find on racks in the lobby, especially for nationwide chains of hotels, which list rates, or ranges of rates, for rooms. Depending on the needs of your group, this rate could be anywhere from a rip-off to a great deal.

2. CORPORATE RATE refers to a rate extended to corporations who place a significant amount of business with the hotel. Usually better than the rack rate, although not always by much.

3. TRANSIENT RATE is a special rate, either corporate or otherwise, which is intended for those traveling alone. This rate generally assumes that the traveler will not expect such extras as, for example, a meeting room. See Group Rate.

4. GROUP RATE is a rate intended for groups, usually meaning that some function space, and perhaps some catered functions, will be needed in addition to sleeping rooms. Depending on the payment method used for these extra services, the group rate can be either better than or not as good as the transient rate. (By the way, the terms "better than or not as good as" as used here, are from the bias of the buyer, not the seller. That is, better

is lower. Obviously from the seller's perspective, just the opposite is true.)

5. SHOULDER SEASON refers to the times of the year between high and low season. This differs by area and can even differ among hotels within an area. For example, in a ski area, the shoulder season is usually just after the skiing peak weather has ended and before the whole place turns to mud. (You may find another "shoulder" just before the ski area's good summer season begins and after the mud has mostly turned to grass.)

6. HIGH AND LOW SEASONS refers to the times of the year when demand is highest for the rooms and lowest. In Phoenix the high season is the winter, and the low season is the summer. In Minneapolis the opposite is true.

7. GOVERNMENT RATE refers to the rate quoted to those who are traveling on government business. This is usually, but not always, available to federal, state and local government employees and sometimes to contractors who are traveling on government business. There is no such thing as a requirement to provide a government rate unless the hotel has entered into a specific agreement with the government entity in question. Nor is there a rule saying that the government rate cannot be extended to those not on official business. The simplest definition is that the government rate is *usually* a discount rate, given because the hotel wants to attract government travelers. This rate might be used as a benchmark to determine how much room there is between here and rack rate.

8. SMURF is a category of business that encompasses groups who generally have a lower budget and thus need lower rates. It is an acronym which stands for Social, Military, Union, Religious, and Fraternal. Note that most of these groups have meetings at which attendance is optional and often paid for out of the individual's own pocket.

9. Single, double, double-double, double-queen, twin, queen, and king. All these terms refer to various configurations and occupancy rates of rooms. A single rate means one occupant, a double rate means two, triple means three occupants and quad means four. (Beyond that, in a normal hotel room, you're in trouble!) A double-double means two double beds, while a double-queen means two queen-size beds, etc. A twin room can mean either two twin beds or, in some (happily rare) cases, that you are being put in a room so small that only one twin bed can fit in it. One other term that applies in this area, and that can be important to your negotiations is *flat rate*. This usually means there is one rate for the room regardless of the number of occupants. Sometimes flat means the same for one or two occupants but additional for more than two.

10. Standard, special, deluxe, etc. About the only thing I can say about these terms is that they define different types (usually different qualities) of rooms within a hotel. There is no such thing as a standard definition of standard, as there is of double vs. queen. Sometimes it refers to size of the room, sometimes to location, sometimes to a combination of the two, sometimes to the floors on which the rooms are located, or to the amenities included in the room. The best thing to learn here is to find out how many categories of rooms there are and how many rooms in each category. Then look at them, and apply your own definitions to them, which may range, instead of from standard to deluxe, from unusable to great.

11. Suites. Again, there are as many definitions of suites as there are inventive minds in marketing and interior design. Some suites have separate parlors, some only sitting areas within the bedroom. Some have two bathrooms, some only one. Some have separate entrances from the hall to parlor and bedroom,

some only one. You have to look at them and define them in terms of your own needs.

12. CONCIERGE LEVEL was discussed briefly in an earlier chapter but is a relatively common practice now among larger chain hotels. It refers to a special area, perhaps the top two floors, of the hotel, where the rooms have special amenities, such as robes, special soaps, turn-down service, etc., which are not available to rooms in other sections of the hotel. They also often have a special lounge and sometimes separate check-in with a special host or hostess, sometimes including free or "honor bar" beverages in the evening and continental breakfast in the morning. There is, of course, normally an extra charge for these rooms. Another point to keep in mind is that access to these rooms is sometimes limited by means of special keys, so not everyone can get to the rooms, even for a visit.

Had enough about sleeping rooms? Remember that all of the above terms can apply *within* one hotel. Let's move on to define some conference or meeting room terms.

CONFERENCE ROOMS

(See Chapter 7 for the illustrations of room setups discussed below.)

1. ROUNDS refers to round tables, of various sizes, which are placed in a room at intervals to provide groupings of from four to ten people. They are best used where you want to have discussions in small groups, inter-mixed with plenary discussions to summarize or share the results of the small discussions. This is also the most common setup for banquets.

2. CLASSROOM STYLE refers to the setup most commonly used for training sessions where the most prevalent style of communication is front to back and where the trainees need to take

notes. It consists of tables facing front, with chairs behind them. The tables can be six or eight feet in width and are usually either 18" or 30" deep. Normal seating is three people to a six-foot table, or four to an eight-foot table. If you need more elbow room than this, be sure to so specify. Front of the room setup here can also vary, from a head table, to a standing podium, to a head table elevated from the rest of the room, or several combinations of these. Be sure to specify what you need for the speaker(s).

3. SCHOOLROOM means the same thing as classroom style, defined above.

4. THEATER is the most economical setup, both in terms of space used and cost of setup. It consists of chairs facing front with no tables. Sometimes there can be armrest tables such as you may have used in school. This arrangement is OK for a brief lecture-type presentation but stifling if the group has to be there very long.

5. HOLLOW SQUARE consists of tables placed in a pattern forming a square with a hole in the middle. Chairs are then placed around the outside of the square. This is good for discussions among "equals" but is not good if the group is very large because the hole in the middle becomes a chasm, cutting off communication.

6. RECEPTION is sometimes known as SRO or standing room only. This is for cocktail parties, receptions and similar functions. Guests are expected to stand and to circulate. There are only perhaps a few small tables for food and beverages and for the few who insist on sitting, and perhaps carts to hold used plates or cups.

These are only some of the many available options for room setup in a hotel or conference center (but will suffice for the purposes of this chapter) that illustrate some of the choices you must consider when negotiating for space and rates.

Why are different room setups a factor in negotiations? Because each setup carries with it a different cost to the hotel and therefore a difference in the potential profit available in its sale to you.

PROFIT CENTERS

Hotels basically have three cost centers: rooms, meals and meeting space. Ideally, all three will show a profit, but the most profit is through the sale of sleeping rooms. The second-best profit center for hotels is meals (which includes beverage service), and last is the sale of meeting space. In fact, meeting space cannot be sold separately in many hotels more than thirty days in advance of the planned date for a function. This policy makes it difficult to plan a local party, but the reason for it is that meeting space is essential to the sale of sleeping rooms for groups, so it is reserved for that purpose. It follows, therefore, that if your sleeping room rate is lucrative enough to the hotel, your meeting space can be free.

SLEEPING ROOMS. Let's look first at the most profitable item, sleeping rooms. Most hotels establish in their marketing plan both a target average rate and a target occupancy rate. If you as a salesperson can exceed both, obviously you will be a hero. If you as a meeting planner are willing and able to allow the hotel to charge you more than the average rate, you should also be a hero to them and should therefore expect the *best*, both in terms of service and types of rooms made available to you.

However, in the real world, that's not usually what's happening. You as a planner need to save dollars on sleeping rooms, either so you have more money for other conference functions, such as meals or speaker fees or whatever, or so you can attract more attendees who will be paying for sleeping rooms "out of pocket", or often for both reasons. So, knowing the twin goals of the hotel, high average rate and high average occupancy, how can you deal?

I suggest you first need to do some serious study of what I call the market. Know the area where you want to go and what its peak and "valley" (another term for low) seasons are. Try to find out what your competition in the city or area is for the time period you want. The local convention and visitors bureau will be glad to help you out here, or you can simply ask the hotels with whom you are talking who else will be in the area when you want to be. If there is a "city-wide", meaning a convention using most space available in the entire city, it usually means you can forget bargain rates. If you can move your meeting just one week in either direction, you may have a much easier time obtaining a favorable rate. Another twist here, however, is that if the "city-wide" is paying a top rate, and if the hotel in question has enough room and meeting space left for your group, you can perhaps benefit. This is because the average rate has already been satisfied, and probably the occupancy rate has been boosted, so your small budget rate meeting is all gravy to the hotel.

Another twist here is to consider the type of city you are using. If you are in one of the two prime months for conventions, either May or October, you may need to avoid the primary convention cities altogether. Cities such as San Francisco, Chicago, New York, Washington, D.C., Los Angeles, Orlando, New Orleans (and several others) are very popular spots for conventions. If you only have a small meeting, why not consider staying away from the major convention spots and look instead at what is known as a second tier (or even third tier) city? Places without convention centers or without major tourist attractions may more easily accommodate you and may, in fact, be better for your group as they are easier to handle from a visitor's point of view (perhaps safer too!).

What about the concept of peak and valley, and shoulder rates? How much difference is there between them? It essentially depends again on the market, which is often affected by the weather. If the differences are extreme, such as in Arizona, the differences in rates are also. If, on the other hand, the weather is not very different year-round, as in San Francisco, the concept of peak and valley is almost non-existent. In San Francisco the primary determinants of market are the tourist season, when children are out of school, and whatever conventions are booked, which can vary from year to year. I find that even though I want nothing to do with "rack rates", the brochures issued by chains can be a valuable source for documenting seasonal rate patterns and dates when they become effective. I recall one brochure (happened to be in Arizona) that quoted the rate for April 15th at $129 per night, but effective April 16th, the rate became $29!! Obviously this particular hotel considered that there was no shoulder; the rate plummeted directly from the peak to the valley floor.

Peak and valley also change over time. I know of an ocean resort on the east coast where the season used to have a shoulder from Memorial Day to July 4, and from Labor Day to October 1. Because of changes in population, popularity of the resort, etc., the shoulder now begins in April, ends on Memorial Day, doesn't pick up again until September 15, and now ends on November 1. This means the peak season has expanded over the years by five to six weeks per year.

As I mentioned earlier, seasonal rate patterns vary by area, so you might expect that northern areas that are not ski areas would have peak seasons in the summer. Similarly, southern areas would be expected to display opposite patterns. Of course, since meeting planning is never simple, there are exceptions. Take Orlando, as an example. School is out during the summer, so many families take the kids to Disney World then, meaning the summer valley isn't as deep in Orlando as in Miami.

Other than seasonal and other market factors, what are other points to consider? When looking at average rate remember that this is calculated for all types of rooms in the hotel. Suites are priced higher than junior suites, which may be higher than doubles, which are in turn higher than singles. Ocean-front, or top-floor rooms may be higher than lower-floor or city-facing rooms. What types of rooms do you need and how many of each? Check the number of rooms of each type available for sale, and try to determine where your group fits in the scheme of things. If you need mostly suites or other top-rate rooms, you will have to pay top dollar. If, on the other hand, you need mostly single standard rooms, you can expect to "deal". Suppose you need 90 percent singles, should you try for a flat rate so the 10 percent who bring their spouses don't have to pay extra? Sounds like maybe you can, but think about it. Should you tax the 90 percent to benefit the 10 percent? What if you told the hotel, "Don't give me a special deal on the doubles, I need your bottom rate on singles"? You may save a dollar or two on the single rooms, making the majority of your participants happy, and the 10 percent with spouses may not care about paying extra anyhow.

If the situation is different, and you need to attract married people to your convention but you will be stealing a weekend from them, it might benefit you to get a flat rate so more married attendees will make the meeting a mini-vacation and boost your attendance. Double rates, by the way, are usually very negotiable. Think what it costs the hotel to have an extra person in the room—a few towels and some extra water and soap. In exchange, more money is spent in restaurants and the gift shop, the bar and perhaps elsewhere.

What about suites? How many do you "need"? (No one *really* needs a suite; we just want them to feed our egos.) The standard rule of thumb says one free room per fifty, meaning for every fifty rooms you rent, you get one free. Going further, the hotel policy may allow you to convert free rooms to suites on a two-to-one ratio, for every two rooms "earned" you can have one suite. If you have 100 rooms per night, you are entitled to one free suite. Fine. But consider for a moment how many suites are in the hotel and how many rooms. Suppose you have 500 rooms and 10 suites; this means one per 50, or probably not much room for begging beyond the "rule of thumb". But now suppose the hotel has 30 suites, and 500 rooms. Normally the suites are the last rooms sold because they are the most expensive, so since the ratio of suites to rooms is relatively high, there are liable to be unoccupied suites just sitting there. The number one rule in hotels is that there is nothing more perishable than a room, meaning you cannot possibly sell last night's vacant room. It's worse than a three-week-old tomato. At least you can make sauce from that; all you make from last night's room is headaches for the accountant. If you need some extra suites, examine the situation in the hotel and try for it. All they can do is say no.

While I'm on the subject of perishability, I also learned never to apologize for a short-term booking request. Some hotels will be sold out, sure, but if you find one with leftover rooms two weeks from your meeting date, you can expect a salesperson who is eager to sharpen a pencil. I don't recommend this approach for a large meeting, of course, but if you have to do short-term business, look at it as an opportunity, not a problem.

I could go on for volumes talking about various twists and turns involved in pricing of sleeping rooms, but perhaps this is enough to give you a flavor of the card game you're involved with without boring you to tears.

MEALS. Let's look now at another aspect of your meeting needs, namely meal functions. Will you have any? Remember I said there are three cost centers involved, and the hotel would like to make money on all of them if possible. So if you are going to have three banquets, two cocktail parties, a theme party and other planned meal functions, your business is potentially much more profitable than if you want only coffee twice a day. (Unfortunately, as most of my meetings were for a government agency, my business tended to be on the poor side of the ledger.)

But given that you will want at least some meal service, how can you bargain to get "the best deal"? There is not as much negotiability here as there is in the sleeping room rate. Although it may seem terribly exorbitant to pay $15.00 for a chicken lunch you can get for $8.50 in the restaurant, you need to factor in the extra costs involved in setting up the function room for your group, bringing in special waiters, special handling needed to feed everyone at once, and several other factors that make conference meals expensive. The reason planners will pay these prices is that for their group and their meeting objectives, it's worth it. Maybe you get more informal networking; perhaps you save time by not turning people loose on their own for lunch. Whatever the reason, I think it's important to know you will be paying a premium for this service and to analyze whether it serves your needs to do so.

As a simple example, let us say you are paying $1.75 per

cup for coffee in the meeting room (plus the ubiquitous service charge and tax, of course). Your option is to turn people loose to go to the hotel restaurant or elsewhere to get their own. Conservatively, that will take at least 30 minutes, probably more like 45. If you serve coffee in the meeting room you can resume your meeting in 15 minutes. Assume further that you have 25 people in attendance and that they each earn an average salary of $15 per hour. If you save 30 minutes for 25 people, you have saved 12.5 hours at $15 per hour, or $187.50. Your coffee only costs you $43.75, so your net savings by paying that exorbitant $1.75 is $143.25. See what I mean?

Since I do not arrange for that many meal functions in my meetings, I will be the first to admit that I am not the foremost expert at bargaining for meal functions. Nevertheless, I have learned a few things that may help you.

First is that hotel meals are much too elaborate for what you really need. Unless if your group has been spoiled by earlier meetings with five-course luncheons, a soup, salad and sandwich buffet can serve just fine. The key is to remember that you want your group to be awake for the afternoon session; so don't overfeed them. Cut out the dessert and you save $4.00 per person. You'll probably give them a cookie for the afternoon coffee break anyhow, or at least you can if you don't buy lunch dessert. Which would be more noticeable to your group, an unexpected "treat" at the break, or a routine dessert after lunch?

Similarly, check the size of the entrees at both lunch and dinner. Maybe you don't need the ten-ounce sirloin. I once cut the prime rib size from ten ounces to six ounces and saved enough to provide wine for everyone with dinner. I received no complaints from anyone about the portion size but many thanks for the "extra touch" of wine with dinner.

Be careful with hors d' oeuvres also. It's easy to order a

"veggie tray" and think you're providing nice healthy food at a low cost, but check the consumption and see if what you are paying for is eaten. The cheese tray is often wasted. On the other hand, if you buy the $2.00-per-piece jumbo shrimp, you can rest assured that they will all be gone, probably within the first 30 minutes of the two-hour reception. Ask yourself what your purpose is in providing snacks. Is it to feed people dinner so they don't have to eat later, or is it to give them something to nibble on while they talk? If it's the latter, forget the shrimp and go for something less elaborate.

Another tip on the snack service is not to put out all the items at once. Use smaller trays and replenish them, so you don't have the gourmands of the group loading their plates five high at the outset, leaving late comers with nothing to eat, or breaking your budget by making it necessary to reorder when you shouldn't have to.

Yet another point I like to make is to suggest you depend on the catering department to help you stay within your budget and still look good. Professionals know what they do best for a group, and it may well be chicken instead of steak. Remember that if you make them look good, you look good too, for choosing them and for choosing the nicely served meal. (I learned this the hard way once, when I insisted that a hotel serve Veal Oscar to a group of 150, even though they begged me to reconsider and said the veal didn't hold up well for a group that size. It was a disaster!)

Finally, be aware of hotel rules when you buy a steamship round of beef. You know your group won't eat it all, but what happens to the leftovers? Do they end up in the employee cafeteria, at your expense, or can you negotiate to have it carved and served as roast beef sandwiches in the president's suite for the board meeting lunch the next day? There are other similar "leftover prone" items, including turkey and ham, which you can use creatively to save money, if you remember to think of it.

But don't go overboard saving money at the expense of boring your people or appearing "cheap". I once read a planner's account of how he had reused the steamship round for four different functions in one weekend, thinking "what a good boy am I", no doubt. My thought, instead, was Yucch! I'm tired of the roast beef already!

My thoughts on meal planning can really be summed up as follows: go light, be creative, and listen to your hosts.

MEETING SPACE. The final cost center for your meeting needs is that of meeting space. The number and size of meeting rooms you need will have a definite impact on your ability to bargain for rates in all categories. If you have 500 people and need only one room theater style, you're in clover. But if you have 45 people, and you need a plenary session for 45 in the morning, a separate room for lunch for 45, then three breakouts in the afternoon, you can be in for some trouble if you expect to get your meeting space for free. Remember that the hotel is a carefully designed package, and its management is trying to balance meeting space and sleeping rooms, so if you exceed your "fair share", you will be expected to pay for it.

Here's another "fair share" example. It's easier for you to have a room on a 24-hour basis so materials don't have to be picked up after each day's session. But this keeps the hotel from using that room for an evening function such as a dinner or reception. If they lose the meal function, who helps their profit line? Answer: you. So if you *really* need the 24-hour basis, and unless the hotel is nearly empty and can accommodate the request without lost business, you must expect to pay for the room somehow, either through meeting room rental or higher sleeping room costs.

Room setup differences cost different amounts. Theater style takes less space, and requires less furniture and less labor than conference style. Also, conference style requires linens to transform those awful plywood tables into lovely pieces. All of it costs money, so expect your bargaining position to be less favorable the higher the cost of your room setup.

BARGAINING

Now we have reviewed all the basic aspects of a meeting in a hotel or conference center. We could discuss such things as use of the golf course, tennis fees, etc., but suffice to say the more money your meeting can put in a hotel, however you do it, the more they will like you. Common sense, isn't it?

So now it's time to bargain. I have only three points to make here.

1. Make sure you end up with what you bargained for. There can be many a slip between what a salesperson promises and what you end up getting billed for. Rather than cover it in detail here, I will refer you ahead to Chapter 18, on Billing and Payment. Read it before you begin to negotiate.

2. Don't start haggling until you have made all your needs clear. It's not fair to squeeze out the last dollar from sleeping rooms, then try to squeeze again for meeting space, and conclude by asking for "just one more favor", a few free suites for the board. You want to do the best you can for your group, but there is a wonderful network out there, and you don't need the reputation of being impossible to deal with to precede you to the next hotel.

3. This point is one I'm sure you have heard before, if you

have been anywhere near a course or book on negotiations. As I said earlier, there are dozens of books on negotiations, so if you haven't read one, please do. Anyhow, the point I want to reiterate is, try to negotiate to a "Win-Win" position. Don't try to "beat your opponent", or you may create an opponent out of a friend. This is supposed to be the hospitality industry, but don't abuse the hospitality. The general rule in the hotel industry is that it's much easier to resell to a satisfied customer than to find and sell to a new one. It works both ways. It's a whole lot easier to call and say, "It's me again, can you do for me what you did last year?", if you, in turn, had done something for your hotel negotiator last year. Take what you need and insist on what you deserve, but don't get greedy.

10

Ethics and "Freebies"

▭▷ Perhaps a few words should be said here about accepting goods or services ("freebies") in the course of doing business. I have already talked about getting free suites, free conference rooms, discounted this and that. Where does it end, and is there anything we shouldn't try to get free?

Perhaps more than any other professional, the meeting planner is put in a position of being offered both goods and services (especially the latter) free. The temptations are great, and the practices are ever expanding, to the point where this issue is becoming a concern in the hospitality industry. You need to decide on a point beyond which you will *not* accept these offers, or you run the risk of ruining your ability to function. What is that point? My attempt here is not to preach but to raise some of the points you should consider in setting your own code of ethics.

First of course, you need to know the rules of your own organization. It may be that acceptance of any item of value from a vendor or potential vendor, for reasons good or bad, is strictly prohibited. This is the case in some government agencies, for example, both federal and local. But what if this is not the case, or you are working as an independent planner? I believe there should be an over-riding rule that if there is no opportunity for the vendor to do business with you, *or* if acceptance of the item offered would interfere with your ability to objectively make purchasing decisions, the gift should be refused.

Let's look at some of the situations you will encounter to illustrate my points. What are some of these terrible temptations?

FAM TRIPS

This is a term that derives from the longer term "familiarization trip". It describes a fairly common practice in the hospitality industry of bringing groups of planners to a city or single hotel for the purpose of selling the attributes and services of that location as the site of future meetings. Usually included are all meals, lodging, tours, cocktails, airfare—truly an all-expenses paid trip. The costs of these range from nothing up to perhaps a few hundred dollars. The duration is normally from three to five days. Spouses or guests are sometimes included.

FAM trips can greatly aid you in making intelligent choices about meeting sites without any, or at least very little cost to your organization. Besides, they are *fun*! So why not go along? Well, applying my rules outlined above, I say you should not go on a FAM trip unless you have a real chance of putting a meeting in the host destination within a reasonable time period. So if you can't meet offshore, don't go on a FAM trip to Hawaii.

Well, what's a reasonable time period? That is a matter of how you book your meetings. For me, it means about three years. Most of my meetings are booked with less than six months lead time, and given the amount of destruction that occurs in a short period of time in hotels (it's amazing how we travelers can trash a beautiful property), I don't trust what I see to last more than three years. So if I can't meet there in three years, I don't go. But some meeting planners need to book meetings as many as ten years ahead. In that case, obviously, my time period would not make sense.

There are those who feel you shouldn't go on a FAM trip unless you definitely know you will be meeting in the city visited. I do not agree with that for the reasons stated in earlier chapters on exhibits and negotiations. I *never* know for certain that I will be meeting in a particular city until I see what the competition is offering in two or three other cities at the same time.

If you do go on FAM trips, however, I feel you should abide by certain rules of conduct. Remember that the purpose of the trip is to educate you as to the possibilities available in the location. So please participate in all planned events. If you never need a convention center, go ahead and tour it with the group anyhow, and don't be negative about it because the small elegant hotel you are particularly interested in will probably be boring to some other member of the group. Also, please be on time. FAM trips are usually rather hectic, so showing up late for a morning event can ruin the schedule for the entire day. This is not to say you shouldn't have fun. The hosts want you to enjoy yourself. It's fine to have fun at the parties, but please cooperate as well on the business portions of FAM trips.

SITE INSPECTION TRIPS

These are similar to FAMs but are custom designed for either you, or you and other colleagues from your organization, to look for a spot for one meeting. Once again the cost can be nothing, discounted, or full price. Which should you pay? Again my rule applies. If you can use the place, and it won't interfere with your judgment, accept the free or discounted rate, *provided* that you really need the trip. If you go on a FAM trip to Phoenix in the spring, then return in the fall of the same year to look again at the same hotels, I begin to doubt the need for the trip. Another factor involved is accepting different levels of "favor" from two or more different properties during the same trip. If you are looking at three hotels, and you stay in a free room at two of them but in a free suite with champagne at the third, will your judgment be swayed? It gets very difficult to honestly say no when you are walking on the red carpet. One rule some planners follow is to stay only in the category of room that will be used by the majority of the group for which they are shopping.

I don't want to overstate the negatives of site inspection trips. That is, there are times when you need to make repeated trips to a location, even after you have booked it. If you are booking several years out, for example, you may want to make it part of the deal that the property will be inspected by you at regular intervals (every eighteen months?), with the understanding that certain standards must be maintained or the deal is off. Or you may need to visit the property about six months out, to plan menus, go over all plans and make sure that agreements made five years ago are still understood. The point is that these trips are obviously business related and made not for your pleasure but for the good of your group.

INCENTIVE TRIPS OR PRIZES

Another temptation you will encounter is the granting of trips or other items, including television sets or stereo equipment, in exchange for meetings booked. Many suppliers feel this whole practice is unethical, but it must work because several organizations are doing it. It works somewhat like the frequent-flyer programs offered by airlines that qualify you for free or upgraded travel after you have flown the specified number of miles. In the case of meetings, the prize is usually based on the number of room nights booked, or meetings booked, within a specified time frame. I feel that if you can convince yourself that the reason you booked the meeting at that property is that it is the best available choice for your group, go ahead and take the bonus. But if you are booking the meeting there so you get to take a vacation to Mexico, think again.

DOOR PRIZES

Many trade shows or conferences offer door prizes as an incentive to get you to attend or to get you to stop by a particular booth. The reason for this is to make sure they get a chance to book your business. So if you win a trip in exchange for leaving a business card, do it! You had the same chance as everyone else, so you won it fair and square. Ah, but there's a caveat here. If you can't book business, don't stop by the booth with the door prize. You are wasting both your time and theirs and violating the spirit of the door prize offering. If you must stop by, politely refuse the chance to enter the contest. I know it sounds altruistic, but think how surprised they will be to encounter a planner without his or her hand out!

PERSONAL FAVORS

Now we're getting into some very sticky ground. Here we're talking not about *accepting* favors, but *soliciting* them. You plan to travel out of town for the weekend on a strictly pleasure basis. You know there's a chain property in your destination city, and you don't want to pay rack rate (who does?). So you call your friendly sales representative in the chain's regional sales office and ask him to intercede on your behalf. Fair or foul?

Hate to be a spoilsport, folks, but I think it's a close call. Can the chain or individual property benefit from this favor? Without biasing your judgment? Have you ever done a favor for the salesperson you are asking, such as introducing him or her to new sales leads? Will you do an honest site inspection of the site you are visiting in exchange for a discount? If you are answering the wrong questions no, then you are violating your personal code of ethics (or at least mine).

NO-SHOWS

I'm changing gears now, to talk about *not* accepting a free service, like a lunch for example, when you had previously agreed to attend. For some reason it seems that some planners feel no qualms about backing out on such an agreement at the last minute and without even notifying the host of their change of plans. Just two horrible examples:

1. A hotel from Hartford, Connecticut hosted a breakfast in Washington, D.C., with the intent of selling the Hartford hotel. Twenty-five planners had accepted the invitation. Three of us showed up! It was hard to say which of us, the planners or the host, was more embarrassed, but I know who was out the money.

2. A state delegation of hotel salespeople hosted a luncheon, again in Washington, to sell the state as a potential meeting site. About 100 guests attended, but there were 32 no-shows. That's almost 25 percent! That in my mind is unethical. We all have to make last minute changes to our plans from time to time, but not 25 percent of us at the same time. How would you feel if that percentage of invited guests to your daughter's wedding didn't show up and didn't tell you? By the way, when we left the luncheon the badges prepared for the no-shows were still prominently displayed on the registration table, so we all know

who the guilty parties were for that occasion. And we do care. Networks work not only between planners and between suppliers but across the lines as well.

Perhaps that is the bottom line on ethics for meeting planners. Given the many opportunities available, you can gorge yourself on goodies in the short term, but if you plan on being in the profession for a while, you will eventually be starved out by your own reputation. Don't let it happen to you.

11

Materials Development

✏️ Now that you have completed all the details of planning for your conference space, exhibits, location and participants, and you have at least a tentative agenda, it's time to get to work. Not that what you have done in planning so far is not work, but it is a different type of function, one unfortunately seen often by "managers" as not very difficult, or even fun. Developing conference materials is almost universally considered difficult. So difficult, in fact, that it is often avoided like the plague. The materials may not even be there when the meeting or conference is held or, developed in a crisis atmosphere, they may be less than they should be.

So how do you avoid this? My suggestion is to plan backwards. That is, start with the dates of the conference and work backwards toward where you are now. As you go, list the things that must be done but in reverse order. (As an example, if shipping completed materials to the conference site needs to be done

one week in advance, then the materials must be complete eight days in advance.) When you finish, you may determine that you should have started development three weeks ago! Then you work forward through the task list(s), checking for items you may have missed or forgotten and find you cannot possibly do everything in time for the conference. Now you are at a point where those who are involved in the conference will listen to you when you try to tell them it's time to begin material development.

The above is stated somewhat facetiously, but in reality you will often find yourself, when you take the time to do some detailed planning about materials development, in a surprisingly tight time frame. You can, of course, try to identify places where you can shorten the time frames needed to accomplish certain functions but only after you have taken the time and effort to scope out the total job. Another way to shorten the time frame needed is to reduce the size of the job. This can mean either deciding you need (or can survive with) fewer materials than you at first planned or, more realistically, assigning the development job to different groups or committees.

To illustrate this division of labor, I have supplied, in the next six pages, task lists for six committees I used once in putting together a conference. The committees included Program, Advertising, Exhibits, Awards, Social and Oversight. As you would expect, many tasks were to be completed concurrently. There were also several points at which the committees had a need for "touching base" with other committees. These points have been marked with an asterisk (*). It was up to the oversight committee to see to it that items or decisions needed by different committees were there on a timely basis.

ADVERTISING COMMITTEE

Task	Plan	Actual
1. Write news release	10/12	_____
2. Clear release with board	10/15	_____
3. Write newsletter article	10/17	_____
4. Design planner solicitation	11/2*	_____
5. Order printing of solicitation	11/9	_____
6. Send planner solicitation	11/16	_____
7. Write newsletter	11/16*	_____
8. Place news release	11/16*	_____
9. Mail info on guest program	11/16*	_____
10. Design flyer	11/30*	_____
11. Order flyer	12/7	_____
12. Distribute flyer to members	12/19	_____
13. Write newsletter article	12/19*	_____
14. Design second planner solicitation	1/4*	_____
15. Print and send second letter	1/11	_____
16. Write newsletter article	1/16*	_____
17. Mail invitations to non-members	1/23	_____
18. Receive ad copy	1/25*	_____
19. Plan final program	1/25*	_____
20. Prepare and issue media announcement	2/1	_____
21. Order final program	2/25*	_____
22. Write newsletter article	2/28*	_____
23. Pick up final program	3/1	_____

PROGRAM COMMITTEE

Task	Plan	Actual
1. Plan seminar content	10/12	_____
2. Design preliminary agenda	10/12*	_____
3. Decide on keynote speaker	10/19*	_____
4. Prepare descriptions of seminars	10/26*	_____
5. Select seminar leaders	11/16*	_____
6. Decide on speaker fees	11/30	_____
7. Send letters to speakers	12/7	_____
8. Arrange for printing of seminar materials	1/26	_____
9. Determine AV equipment needs	2/8	_____
10. Order signs for seminars	2/8	_____
11. Arrange for AV equipment delivery and pickup	2/22	_____
12. Receive signs and materials	3/1	_____
13. Arrange for hosting speakers	3/1	_____
14. Plan and print agenda for board meeting	3/8	_____

EXHIBIT COMMITTEE

Task	Plan	Actual
1. Design exhibit booth setup	10/12*	_____
2. Develop solicitation letter	10/19	_____
3. Send solicitation letter	11/16	_____
4. Plan door prize programs	12/7	_____
5. Prepare booth rules and instructions for door prizes	12/14*	_____
6. Send confirmation letters requesting payment	1/11	_____
7. Receive money for booths and ads	1/19*	_____
8. Order booth signs	2/1	_____
9. Print list of door prizes	2/8*	_____
10. Receive booth signs	3/1*	_____
11. Select door watchers	3/8	_____
12. Plan supplier caucus	3/8	_____

AWARDS COMMITTEE

Task	Plan	Actual
1. Determine awards policy	10/12	
2. Solicit awards	10/26	
3. Send confirmation letters to award donors	12/7	
4. Arrange program copy for award donors	12/21*	
5. Select award winners	1/11	
6. Clear selections with board	1/14	
7. Order plaques	2/1	
8. Select committee members to be recognized	2/1	
9. Order committee certificates	2/8	
10. Select speaker for awards banquet	2/8*	
11. Get speaker's gift engraved	3/1	
12. Prepare banquet presentations	3/8	

SOCIAL COMMITTEE

Task	Plan	Actual
1. Plan guest program	10/15*	_____
2. Prepare descriptions, brochures etc. for guest program	10/22	_____
3. Finalize travel arrangements	11/2	_____
4. Plan conference social events	11/16*	_____
5. Solicit event sponsors	11/23	_____
6. Select and hire band	1/11	_____
7. Get tickets, materials for guest program	2/1	_____
8. Choose event sponsors	2/1*	_____
9. Order signs for event sponsors	2/8	_____
10. Plan food functions	2/15	_____
11. Arrange for dinner music	2/15	_____
12. Hold suite upgrade drawing	2/20	_____
13. Select photographer	2/22	_____
14. Arrange details re guest housing and info	3/1	_____
15. Conference	3/17	_____

OVERSIGHT COMMITTEE

Task	Plan	Actual
1. Set committee budgets and plans	10/5*	
2. Set income targets	10/5	
3. Get hotel brochures and registration forms	10/17	
4. Send advisory letter to hotel	10/17	
5. Plan schedule of committee meetings	10/17*	
6. Order T-shirts, lapel pins	10/30	
7. Receive first hotel feedback	1/4*	
8. Receive hotel feedback	1/11	
9. Receive hotel feedback	1/18	
10. Receive hotel feedback	1/25	
11. Receive hotel feedback	2/1	
12. Receive hotel feedback	2/8	
13. Receive hotel feedback	2/15	
14. Arrange speaker accommodations	2/15	
15. Arrange registration table details	2/20	
16. Order ribbons and badges	2/22	
17. Receive hotel feedback	2/22	
18. Receive hotel feedback	3/1	
19. Receive final hotel feedback	3/8	
20. Collect and ship all conference materials	3/8*	
21. Hold tie-down meeting	3/14	
22. Arrange for staff tips	3/14	

For example, if the Advertising Committee needed to send the flyer to the printer on December 1, then the Program Committee needed to get the program details to the Advertising Committee beforehand.

What happens if materials are not, in fact, completed on a timely basis? Then plans need to be changed. Either you get by without some materials, or you change dates. (Or you apply pressure to the lagging group to get the job done.) Carrying forward the same example, if the Program Committee has not determined the keynote speaker by the time the Advertising Committee needs to know, you may have to choose between going to print with a program that says "Keynote speaker to be determined" or paying a premium price to the printer for faster work. Neither of these choices is very good, but one of them must be chosen unless you can get the Program Committee to act in a timely manner.

You will notice on my task lists that I have two date columns, one for planned and one for actual. The tracking of actual vs. planned performance is critical to planning for future similar events. If your track record is poor on this year's conference, you will know that next year's dates will need to be more lenient or next year's resources applied to the task more intensely.

But what if you have to do several meetings, on different subjects, involving different people, and the meeting dates overlap? How can you maintain your sanity? The obvious solution is to develop standards of practice that can be applied to all your meetings, regardless of subject. It may be that not all details of the different meetings are the same, but there are a great many that surely are. For example, shipping dates, printing times, speaker notification lead times, menu planning deadlines, rooming lists, hotel contracts and a host of other meeting material related activities can be standardized into routine task lists. A simplified list of such tasks is given here relating to the planning and conduct of repetitive training courses during a year. Dates are listed in weeks, meaning that −8 is eight weeks before the course date, while +1 is one week after the course.

TO DO	
1. Announce course	−8
2. Receive nominations	−6
3. Choose meeting site	−5
4. Confirm attendance	−4
5. Return hotel contract	−4
6. Ship course materials	−1
7. Conduct course	0
8. Complete course evaluation	+1

With the help of today's technology, you can even develop computerized calendars of "due dates" across meetings (or committees) to allow one meeting manager to track and control many meetings at once. It follows, by the way, that a centralized meeting manager can do a better job of managing many meetings than can be done by many separate part-time meeting managers who each manage one or two meetings per year.

I think the key to successfully developing conference materials is in breaking down the task into as many small routine tasks as you can and then remembering that each small routine task is as important as any major task. Without this recognition, your carefully constructed master plan becomes a house of cards. What good does it do to have professionally prepared handouts if your mail clerk forgets to ship them to the conference site on time?

I like to say that no ordinary individual can build an automobile, but anyone can put a headlight in place. (Given the special tools that Detroit seems to be requiring today for headlight replacement, I may have to change my pet saying.) Anyhow, the point is, do not be overwhelmed by the enormity or seeming "fuzziness" of the task. If you do it only occasionally, take the time to think the whole task through and document each step. If you do it frequently, have a standard list of functions and time frames, and update that list as you experience new or unplanned exigencies.

One other point. While you are developing lists of "to dos," why not have a standard checklist of items that you should pack for each conference? Call it your emergency kit or whatever else you want to, but here's one for you to build from.

Checklist of Items to be Considered in Packing for a Conference

1. Pens and pencils
2. Grease pens or non-permanent ink pens for acetates
3. Magic markers
4. Pointers
5. Scratch paper (note pads)
6. Stapler and extra staples
7. Staple remover
8. Rubber bands
9. Paper clips (both large and small)
10. Chalk and eraser
11. Three-hole punch
12. Scissors
13. Name tags or tent cards for names
14. Copy of correspondence with hotel
15. Personal notebooks
16. Extra agendas
17. Extra evaluations
18. Notebooks or training material (including acetates)
19. Training equipment (projector, recorder, screen, etc.)
20. Masking tape
21. Blank acetates
22. Aspirin, Band-Aids (don't forget paper cuts)

12

Travel Logistics

✎ You have to get to the conference and back again. And, depending on your conference design, you may have a bit of getting to and from during the conference as well. In this chapter I want to address both issues, beginning with getting to and from the conference.

GETTING THERE

In most cases travel to and from a conference entails, at least for some, air travel. Enter confusion! With the deregulation of airlines, we have entered into a world of almost unreal complications in both travel planning and especially in travel cost projections or budgeting.

It is not unusual to pay as much or more to travel to an adjacent state as you would to fly across the country. There are myriad fare structures and almost as many restrictions applying to those structures as there are fares. Advance planning can save you some very important dollars, but in most cases you will have to sacrifice flexibility of travel plans for savings. And you may face the possibility of losing the entire fare paid if you have to change reservations at the last minute. You can wait until the last minute to maximize your flexibility, but you will pay dearly for it. Also, since the introduction of "hub" cities, airline capacity appears to be very fully utilized these days. While this delights the airlines, it leaves you with the very real possibility of not getting a seat if you wait too long.

You also face the problem of trying to get a non-stop flight, as opposed to taking a flight with one or more stops and often a change of plane required. As you might expect, non-stop flights are generally more expensive or at least not as discountable as other flights.

So, if you are trying to establish a budget for your group to go to a conference, good luck! About the best you can do is to make certain assumptions about your participants' travel patterns and advance planning, then develop fares based on those assumptions. For example, if you decide that none of your participants will purchase tickets more than 30 days prior to the conference, then you can eliminate any fares requiring such purchase.

You may have the advantage of being able to dictate your group's travel arrangements, in which case you can be much more sure of your ground in developing a budget. If you are in this situation, I would caution you to consider whether the savings you can achieve are worth the headaches you will get from trying to please all your travelers.

If your group is large enough to qualify, you may benefit from naming a particular airline as your "Official Carrier" or "Convention Airline". This locks in certain discounted fares, which are negotiable. It is not unusual to receive discounts of 40 percent or more off full-coach fare (for those who need or want to wait until the last minute) or 5 percent off the lowest available fare for those who can take advantage of discounted fares. Just as an example of how much difference we are talking about here, two friends of mine recently traveled between San Francisco and southern California. The first planned ahead and paid $58 round-trip between San Francisco and San Diego. The second waited until the last minute and paid $180 one way from Los Angeles (one hundred miles closer) to San Francisco. So discounts can definitely add up! Naming a convention airline also gives you several side benefits, including knowledge of the travel patterns so you can coordinate ground transportation, and also in some cases you have a better handle on how many people will be in attendance at your conference. Most airlines will also give you one or more complimentary seats, either for site inspections or as a reward for seats sold, or both.

There is very little commitment on your part to the airline and no cost to you to do this. Usually about the only requirement the airline makes is that you name them in your conference literature as the official carrier for the event. Obviously if you intend to do this, you need to exercise care in choosing the right airline for your conference setting, or it will do you no good. If your official carrier doesn't have enough "lift" (airlinese for enough flights with enough available seats) from your starting points to your destination, you cannot take full advantage of the opportunities such a move can afford you.

In some cases, you may have to name more than one official carrier for your conference, perhaps one to provide service from the east and north and another to serve your western and southern participants. As long as both airlines know what you are doing, there is nothing unethical or irregular in this.

Another option that may be available to you is to charter an airplane or a bus. If this is a possibility, it would allow you to effectively extend the social portion of your conference in both directions, both prior to and after the "official" activities. It would also make negotiations easier, as charter arrangements are not bound by as many rules and regulations. I am not an expert in this area, as I have made only a few arrangements of this type. It might be worth an investigation if the size and geographic distribution of your group make it feasible.

Regardless of what arrangements you make for travel or whether you just leave travel arrangements to the individual traveler, you need to factor the time needed for travel into your planning for an agenda. If it takes most of a day to get there, you don't want a meeting that starts at mid-day. Also, you should plan on ending the meeting, if possible, at a time of day that allows travel home within a reasonable arrival hour or one requiring travel on the next day. In the latter case, perhaps a "fun" event on the last evening can enhance the whole design of the conference rather than leaving a bad taste because you made them stay over another night.

Another aspect of "getting there" is the ground transportation available at the destination from airport to conference site. Most major airports have limousine service of some type, but it is not always convenient. Perhaps there is scheduled service only every half hour or even every hour. It's wise in such cases to know the alternatives and perhaps consider putting forth some effort to ease the strain of getting there. If your participants are irritable from changing planes, then waiting for a bus ride, then standing in line to register at the hotel, you're in trouble before your meeting even starts.

I mentioned earlier that using an official carrier might make scheduling ground transportation easier. We once found that due to travel patterns of our group, we could provide stretch limousine transportation to and from the airport at less cost than having the participants fend for themselves! This gave a real lift to the meeting, especially since the participants were not seasoned travelers, and most of them had never ridden in a limousine before.

IN AND AROUND

Once you have all your participants on site, the meeting may begin. But your transportation concerns are often not over. You may need to schedule drivers to pick up part-time participants who are VIPs (speakers or otherwise), or you may have events that call for off-site activities during the conference, such as spouse tours, golf outings, or similar functions. Careful timetables are required here, and you may want to do a "dry run" of the route to be traveled before the event to make sure surprises such as road construction are not lurking to ruin your awards banquet or golf tournament tee times.

I have found convention and visitors bureaus to be of help in locating options for ground transportation, but remember that bureaus cannot recommend one member over another unless you have specified certain parameters that cannot be met by all. You may, for example, require rest rooms on all vehicles, which might eliminate some carriers. But in the final analysis, you should negotiate with carriers yourself and check them out just as you would a hotel. Ask for references and use them. Don't get stranded, as I did once, with 37 passengers waiting to go visit Elvis Presley's home at the end of a long and arduous day of technical training, and no bus! The company had gotten the days mixed up, and no one was in the office to deal with the problem. Luckily for me, the firm did have an answering service and quick reaction by them got me a bus only 15 minutes late.

Other points to consider include the availability and cost of optional transportation available to your participants, such as hotel vans or limousines or taxicabs. The more you can help participants enjoy themselves during their free time, the more responsive they will be to what you want them to do during the official conference events. How about bicycle rentals or horse-drawn carriage rides? Are there riverboat rides, helicopter tours, water-taxis, subways or bus transportation? Remember you are going to be looked to for advice on all matters. If you don't know, it may not matter, but if you do know, it will be a plus for your conference and for your career.

Peripheral Activities

▷ In this chapter I want to discuss those events that are not really part of your conference or meeting, but that can have an impact on its success or failure. Included here are spouse programs, cultural events or entertainment offered in the conference city, planned parades or demonstrations that can be a plus or a minus, and so forth. Not included are those "peripheral activities" you plan for your participants, such as banquets. These I cover in the next chapter, under "Social Events".

Often the success of a conference is determined by your ability to draw participants to the site and to keep them there for the duration of all planned events. This in turn is influenced by, among other things, the attractiveness of the conference site or city to family members or friends of the participants, as well as to the participants themselves. No offense intended, but some sites are just a whole lot easier to sell than others. In February, Scottsdale will appeal to more people than will Buffalo (the reverse may be true in August).

But assuming the cities being considered are basically "equal" in terms of their drawing power, it behooves you to do some research into what's happening in the cities other than your conference. If your group likes country music, the London Philharmonic Orchestra's concert on Thursday evening will not attract as many people who are "on the fence" about attending your conference as would a Willie Nelson concert. If your group plays golf, the availability of courses open to them outside your conference hours is important.

Are there several options of interest to spouses, or would they be forced to find their own amusements? Are there activities for children in the area? Do you want children there, or would you prefer to discourage their attendance?

What about the availability of "tie-in" vacations for your group either before or after your conference? For example, Denver is a popular jumping-off place for winter vacations in the mountains. Orlando, for obvious reasons, is a popular spot for families. It's not only what's happening during your event but what can be planned to tie onto your event that may help you raise attendance.

It is a good idea to find out what other conferences or meetings are happening either in your conference center or in areas adjacent. Sales conventions for door-to-door sales forces can be quite "rowdy", at least in terms of noise and elevator and lobby traffic. If noise will interfere with your meeting, you better consider carefully before booking. A factor to consider is whether the hotel will give your group enough attention or whether all their energies will be devoted to serving complicated meeting and social-event needs of another group in the house with you.

What about the accessibility of these peripheral events to your group? If there's a major event of interest to your group at the convention center, how will the group get there and back from your meeting site? Can they shop or eat at non-conference times without a major hassle, or will you have to make special arrangements for non-official transportation?

What are the hours for attractions in the city? Do they conflict with your meeting hours? I once had a group of trainees in a city who were very interested in visiting the palatial home of a local rock star, but our meetings were scheduled to run until after the regular closing hours of the famous attraction. To keep the peace, even though a trip to the mansion was not an official event sponsored by our group, I had to arrange a special tour, with special transportation, at special hours, or I would have had at least a minor rebellion on my hands. (No comments, please, on the taste of my group. It's not important what I like. As a meeting planner, I had to cater to their likes.)

If your group likes baseball, and you're in a town where a major league team plays, will the team be in town when you are? If not, can you adjust your dates to match theirs? If so, can you make sure there is not a conflict between meeting and baseball hours?

Museums, golf courses, famous buildings or statues, theaters or concert halls, or special events such as antique shows and craft shows held in the city during your event can all add to the attractiveness of the city (and to your potential headaches). Take the trouble to find out at least some of what's happening around you, and include this information in your invitation to attend. It can make a big difference in the attendance at your conference and in the attitude of those attending.

14

Social Events

▣ What social events are you planning in conjunction with your meeting? And how will you pay for them, and how will you determine attendance numbers in advance? And what will you do to avoid legal liability given the problems generated by alcohol? And are you sure you really want to be a meeting planner?

Actually, though social events are sometimes extra trouble, it's probably also true that they are generally much more fun to plan than the meeting sessions. And they generally also give you much more opportunity to show some creativity and to explore new ideas. In fact that may be one of the most important goals of your social event planning, to do something different (read "bigger and better") than last year.

Social events, in my opinion, should not be considered peripheral to the conference but an integral part of it. That's why I am handling them separately from the types of activities covered in the previous chapter. Social events are sponsored by your organization. Therefore they should reflect the image your organization wants to put forward and should contribute to the goals of the conference. For example, if a goal of the meeting is to build teamwork, a social event that generated intense competition among factions at the conference would be counterproductive.

I also feel that social events should "build" as you proceed through the conference, so that your biggest, most elaborate event serves as the culmination of the entire conference, with only a wrap-up to be completed after the final social activity. Thus, you should begin with perhaps an informal reception the first night, including some ice-breaking activities, followed perhaps by a game-type interlude the next day (golf tournament, tennis or swimming parties, shopping excursions or city tours), capped by the awards banquet or similar event, if you are having one, on the last evening of your stay.

But let us move to planning an event to illustrate some of the things you need to consider. Let's assume you want an opening reception. You need to plan duration, timing, location, dress code, food, beverages, entertainment, speakers (if any), transportation to and from the event, and how to get a count for your planning purposes. Remembering that the event should serve your conference goals, let us make a few assumptions, as follows.

1. Your group is coming from several locations, and they haven't, for the most part, seen each other since last year's conference.

2. About half the group will be bringing spouses, and you cannot predict the relative numbers of males and females who will be there.

3. You have an option of an indoor or outdoor location, as you would if your conference were to be in the Southwest in the spring.

4. The overall purpose of your conference is to review accomplishments and failures of the past year and to announce priorities and goals for the coming year.

5. The range in age of your participants is from early twenties through sixties.

6. The first session begins on the following day and features a speech by your top executive, which means it is more or less a "command performance".

All of the above information is available to you if you have done your homework on your group. The situations depicted are quite normal for groups both in business and government. All "facts" can also contribute to your event design and should be taken into account, along with perhaps a number of other factors such as any dietary restrictions, either for health or religious reasons, and whether accessibility by handicapped people is a factor for you.

Given the above, assume that most people will be on-site by 5:30 P.M. or so, (we have checked our arrival patterns by researching schedules of our conference airline), and that it will be pleasant weather in the evening because we are in the sunny Southwest. Therefore, we will decide to have an outdoor function, but we will *definitely* have a back-up indoor location reserved for us in case Mother Nature crosses us up. I once had a poolside reception rained out in Scottsdale in June.

Because the event is on a travel day for most participants, we want to have the event on-site in the hotel, so as not to make our participants travel again to some cross-town museum or other venue. (This also eliminates transportation , liability and other problems, but of course we would cope with these if it were for the good of the group, wouldn't we?)

We don't want the event to last too long; the participants may be tired, and we want them up early in the morning. However, it can't be too short because that would make us look cheap. It would also detract from our goal of beginning the conference with some ice-breaking activities. We will run the event from 7:00 P.M. to 9:00 P.M. Because that is the dinner hour for most people and because we want to make it easy for our attendees, we will serve what is known as "heavy hors d'oeuvres" so they can skip dinner if they want to. We don't want to have a dinner per se, both because we want to encourage conversation and intermingling and because we have a limited budget and can afford only one full-blown banquet.

Again because of our limited budget and because we know some of our people will come early and devour all the goodies, we will not put the food out at the beginning. We will instead use butler service, which is less expensive, uses far fewer pieces of the expensive items such as shrimp, and makes it easier for the hotel or other caterer to ration food service to stay within our allotted amounts. To allow those who are truly hungry some nourishment, at least perceived as such, we will have some action stations serving up some tasty morsels that are filling. (These action stations also make it easier to control consumption by early arrivals than if precooked items were all heaped on a platter in the middle.) Because our group is weight and cholesterol conscious, we will have a mixed menu including vegetable greens and white meats along with the traditional heavier items.

Next, to the matter of beverages. We want to provide what our group wants (or thinks they want), and we want to stay within budget and not encourage overconsumption. We can do this by limiting the number of serving stations (not a good idea), by providing a cash bar (depends on the history and expectations of the group), by limiting beverages to less than "hard" liquor, or by several other means. (For example, you could use 80 proof instead of 95 proof gin for martinis.)

Finally, we need to consider speeches and other entertainment. I know, speeches are seldom the same as entertainment, but the "speechers" don't know that. Again, we want to encourage informal conversation, yet we want the group to feel welcomed and together. To encourage the former, we will limit music to background, and to promote the latter, we will have a *brief* welcoming address by some secondary dignitary less awesome than our CEO, perhaps our local manager, acting as "host."

One final point on the subject of informal discussions or visiting. You will need name badges. I know a lot of people don't like them. They make holes if you use pins, they can ruin velvet or other similar materials if you use stick-on badges. They can clash with what you're wearing, and any number of other reasons can be advanced for hating badges. But remember that I said these people haven't seen each other for awhile. It's embarrassing to recognize a face but not remember the name. It's even more embarrassing if the other person knows your name. Believe me, I know because I have a terrible memory for names. I can remember telephone numbers but not names. So give those like me a break and encourage the wearing of badges to all conference events. You can, by the way, use them as a form of identification in place of tickets when you need to make sure that only your group attends a particular reception or dinner.

Now, how do we tie this all together so we have a theme instead of just another cocktail party?

How about a pool terrace Mexican/Southwest buffet? We can serve a variety of filling items that are not very expensive, such as tacos, burritos and the like. We can find a wide variety of "nibblies" to accompany them. For those who are not fond of Mexican food we can provide Southwestern alternatives such as chicken fingers in barbecue sauce, ribs and so on. We can encourage lighter drinking by clever placement of posters or other enticements for cerveza and margueritas; in fact, we might limit the bar to those two items, plus of course some non-alcoholic alternatives.

As to entertainment, we will have strolling mariachis (without the trumpet please) so people can talk easily without shouting. And we will ask our host speaker to keep it down to a few sentences of welcome.

Let's see what we have done to address the issues I laid out at the beginning:

1. Duration—two hours
2. Timing—7:00–9:00 P.M.
3. Location—poolside
4. Dress code—casual (dictated by location, you don't even have to state it)
5. Food—not expensive, but filling and different
6. Beverages—limited, inexpensive and novel
7. Entertainment—background, tied to theme
8. Speakers—only one, very brief
9. Transportation—none needed
10. Count—dictated by next morning's schedule

See, it can be fun, inexpensive, and contribute to the conference goal, all at once. If you're real lucky, you may even have people anticipate the agenda by discussing accomplishments (we all like to brag) and expected goals (we all like to speculate and gossip).

But that's only one event. I'm tired and we haven't even started the meeting yet. I didn't say it was easy, I said it was fun. If you don't enjoy doing things like I've just described, then you better either (a) find a person to whom you can delegate these items, or (b) get out of meeting planning. Social events are part of the territory.

How can you learn about what items are inexpensive and expensive, how many pieces of which to order for how many, which items the particular hotel serves well and which it doesn't, and how to mix all the ingredients to make a successful function? I believe that this is where you need to lean on the hotel or caterer's expertise and advice. Yes, you should know comparative costs of different food items, but these you can check by reading the fixed menus that come as part of every meeting or conference planner's brochure. What you need from the caterer is a list of what they do well and what has proved popular and unpopular with similar groups in the past. Remember that you are dealing with the hospitality industry and that their job first and foremost is to please you. If you do not feel comfortable with the catering manager for your event, you should consider moving it to another site. I believe service is much more important than location. After all, within certain ranges all hotels have beds and meeting rooms. Not all have attentive caring staffs dedicated to making your meeting a success. Therefore, at least the preliminary discussions of meal and related expenses and options should be part of your original negotiations for the conference site. Ignoring this aspect until after the contract is signed can present you with almost insurmountable problems.

As we did for the opening reception, each event should be planned with an eye to the demographics of your group, with the conference theme or goal in mind, and in relation to the other events both preceding and following the event you're now working on. (Another theme breakfast the next morning along Mexican/Southwest lines, for example, is probably not a good idea.)

For those of you who are really "into" this, let's do another event. If this type of thing bores you, I suggest you skip to the next chapter. Anyone still here? Okay, let's do a banquet. For the sake of continuity, let's assume it is the same group for which we did the informal buffet reception. But now we are nearing the end of the conference. We have discussed successes and failures, we have heard the grandiose plans and schemes for the coming year, and we are ready to cap this successful conference with a really big event. Here are some details for planning.

1. There will be awards given for top achievements during the past year.
2. Budget, while not unlimited, is not to interfere with the success of the event.
3. You will precede the dinner with a cocktail reception.
4. There will be one speaker in addition to those speaking about the awards.
5. Dancing will follow the dinner and speeches.

What do these things tell us? First, you don't want heavy hors d'oeuvres at the cocktail reception because you will have a full dinner immediately following. Second, the majority of people will be more interested in dancing than in listening to speeches, so you have to talk to the Awards Committee and tell them to keep it short. Also, a little humor in events such as this never hurts, so suggest some humorous awards in addition to the serious ones (maybe the worst golf score or poorest joke heard at the conference). We have already had a Mexican buffet, so stay away from that as a theme. Dancing usually means a fairly dressy evening as does the tone of the event, so consider the kind of food served so you don't ruin someone's gown. (Spaghetti sauce is a no-no.) You will probably want to begin presentations before everyone is finished with dessert, so stay away from something requiring elaborate service, (and thus distracting) such as Baked Alaska. As long as the band is going to be there part of the time, arrange for dinner music before the dancing. It avoids band setup during dinner service and adds to the ambiance of the evening at relatively little cost.

In keeping with the general tone of the evening, you will probably want a head table. Be careful whom you put there and how you seat those who are there. Also, take care to see that the head table occupants know that they must be there before anyone else can be served, and ask them therefore to be prompt (touchy sometimes, but necessary). The head table will probably be raised, or on risers, as the meeting jargon goes. Be sure that access is easy, so award winners know where to go to accept awards and don't break their backs getting there.

Given the nature of the event, the timing, and the dress code, you most probably will want this dinner to be in the host property, usually the ballroom. Don't overlook, however, other possible alternatives. Perhaps there is a roof-top restaurant closed for the season due to lack of business that can be opened for your group. It would make a lovely setting for the event and may even make the meal cost less because you don't have to create a restaurant as you would in the ballroom. In this case the restaurant is already built, so decorations are easier, and maybe service is even more efficient.

Notice I haven't really mentioned food very much. Just keep the reception light, stay away from staining sauces, and order a simply served dessert. I happen to feel that the food served at an affair such as this is not that important. The *event* is important; people will probably not remember past the next day what the entree was, let alone the accompanying vegetable. Again, I would lean heavily on the catering staff or chef to tell me what would be best for my group and my function. Make it look elegant, let it be served efficiently, make sure it stays hot until it gets to the table, and you have succeeded. One tip I suggest is to have the chef describe the meal in his or her terms and prepare a menu to place on the table at each plate. I say let the chef describe it, because that will turn carrots into "fresh garden delight, prepared with sauce Florentine". I don't know what that is, but I'd rather have it than carrots, even if it turns out to be the same thing. Finally, watch how your meal choice relates to other meal choices made not only at this conference but to the banquet dinner you served last year. While the event is probably similar, you should try to do *something* a little different.

15

Speakers / VIPs

▶ In this chapter I want to cover not the selection of your speakers and VIPs but their "care and feeding" and what it will cost you, in time, in trouble and in actual money.

Any sizeable meeting, whether corporate, association, government or whatever, always has a certain pecking order among attendees. Someone is "in charge", not so much of the meeting (that should be the meeting manager) but in charge of the group that is meeting. It may be the boss, or several layers of bosses. This constitutes one type of VIP. Another category might be the invited guests, perhaps the past president, the retired former boss, a politician whose favor you need, or some other personage who may not have a large or direct involvement with the group or the meeting but who for ceremonial purposes needs some special treatment.

Then you have your speakers, either paid or unpaid, a category of VIPs definitely different from the other two. In addition to their ceremonial VIP status, speakers also have special needs that can affect the success of your meeting. For example, speakers may have specialized audio-visual, room setup or handout requirements that need to be anticipated and met.

In my experience, the latter group may be the easiest to deal with. They are usually experienced conference participants, and though their expectations may at times be extravagant or unreasonable, you can at least find out what they want, need and like, simply by asking.

The second group, the invited guest, generally expects what last year's guest received. That is, a past president will, of course, know how last year's past president was treated and will probably be satisfied to receive that level of special treatment (but not any less!).

The "bosses", however, can range from no problem at all to major headaches for you before, during and after the meeting. A chief executive who wanted absolutely nothing special, not even a suite, said to me on arrival at the conference, "Tell me what I'm supposed to do to help the meeting." (We need more like that!) I have also heard about (thankfully *not* experienced) this ridiculous pecking order; (1) The size of the suites assigned, and (2) the quality of liquor provided in each suite had to be carefully orchestrated to coincide with the various levels of "chieftain" being served!

The first thing to do in this area, if you are coming into an organization with a conference history, is to determine what that history is. This is not to say that you must do everything that was done in the past. However, if you change, it's usually OK to raise the level of special treatment, but if you're going to lower it, you better have a very good reason (i.e. the hotel doesn't have enough suites to upgrade all the bosses) and you better clear the change prior to the conference to avoid on-site unexpected disappointments and confrontations.

Also consider, of course, before you change anything, what this is going to cost. The old saying about "no free lunch" definitely applies here. Hotels don't give away suites because they like your smile. They do it because they like your business, which means they are making a profit. In other words, what you get in free suites will probably cost you in food functions or meeting space rental. And remembering what I said above about the difficulty of lowering the level of special treatment, you'll want to think twice about taking something easily offered this year, because you may be obligating your organization to provide that service in future years at what could become very expensive rates.

The key, I think, is to remember *why* you are providing special services to your VIPs. It's not so much how extravagant you can be but that you are recognizing them as being "special" at your meeting and worthy of being rewarded in some token manner for their role.

For purposes of discussion, let us assume you are not coming into a situation with a history but are beginning a set of conferences that will be continued over the years, the first annual. In this case you are, in a sense, creating the conference history or setting the mold others will be obliged to follow or try to top.

What are some of the amenities you can consider, and how do you determine which are the more desirable to your VIPs? Which can be obtained at the lowest cost, in dollars and aggravation, and which will have the most impact both in terms of pleasing your VIPs and in pointing out their special role to the other participants at your meeting?

Let's start at the airport (or even earlier). How about first-class or business-class air travel? Relatively high cost, perhaps high impact on the VIP, but not seen at all by the other participants. Limousine travel from the airport? Relatively easy to arrange, at least for a few people, usually fun for the VIP, and visible to at least some of the conference participants. Suites, concierge level rooms, amenities in the rooms? In general, all of these are not too hard to arrange and usually pleasing, maybe even expected by VIPs, but have very little visibility. In fact, being on a concierge level can mean that your VIPs cannot be seen by others. Also, with access to that area of the hotel limited, VIPs sometimes can't invite guests to their lounge without involving an embarrassing system of charges, etc.

Plaques or certificates are often given. They offer high visibility at low cost, but how much value do they have for the VIP? Would you rather have another plaque or a suite? Similarly, seating at the head table gives visibility, at virtually no financial cost, but sometimes at the cost of actual discomfort to the VIP.

One trick I learned from a hotel salesperson, who rose to the top of his trade, was to spend a little time finding out something personal about the individual VIP, in order to make the special treatment meaningful. He had learned from the VIP's secretary, for example, that the VIP did not drink. So instead of wine and cheese, she was presented with two cute toys to take to her two grandchildren. The note accompanying the gift said something like, "Hope your stay with us is pleasant, and your grandchildren will be happy to see you when you get back." This gesture took very little time, probably cost less than the wine and cheese, and may have brought the whole meeting back to that hotel next year, because the VIP had a special memory of the treatment she got. Applying that to your role as a planner, you may be remembered as a "real pro", even if the steak is burned, because you made your VIP happy.

Finally, a word of caution. I don't believe we should get

carried away with trying to provide these special services. Again, they cost money and are really not necessary. A little differentiation from the other participants will probably serve as well as a major distinction. Remember that you are serving not only the VIPs but the entire group. If you get too many free suites, you may have to sacrifice the Danish at your coffee break. Don't lose perspective.

The cost of VIP treatment must also be factored into your conference budget. Free guests are not really free. You may be able to get the room without charge, but remember always that VIP meals, transportation, perhaps spouse expenses as well, must be figured out *prior to* setting your registration fees. Tacking on extra guests after you have established your fee structure and budget can very easily mean the difference between a conference ending up in the black or the red.

16

Last Minute Crunch

✏ As the time for your conference draws near, it sometimes seems that everything is happening at once and that all your plans have been for naught. There are so many things still to be done and so little time in which to do them. Some pop up at the last minute, but many can be anticipated and taken care of ahead of time.

What kind of things jump out of the bushes at you? I am referring to last minute requests for room changes, either in sleeping rooms or meeting rooms; peripheral functions, whether committee meetings or social events; missed handouts; changes by the hotel without notification; bad weather; strikes; speaker illness; demands for special meals because of diet or religious reasons; meal guarantees; functions that run late, interfering with other events; lost registration fees; missed airplanes; audio-visual failures; electrical outages; fire drills. The list is endless. Given such a litany of lurking disasters, why did you allow yourself to be put in this position? Remember when you thought meeting planning was glamorous?

Well, in truth, it still can be. The list above is only of *potential* problems; they haven't happened yet, and certainly not all of them will. Furthermore, they can all be handled; yes, even the weather, to a certain extent. The key is anticipation. For each possibility, you need to have considered "what if?", and come up with a backup or plan of action. Let's run through a few just for examples.

SLEEPING ROOMS. What is your policy regarding late registration? Will the hotel allow latecomers to register at the same conference rate? If not, do you have provisions for a backup or overflow property near your main facility? Don't wonder whether this will happen, assume it will. Someone is always going to decide at the last minute that he either *has* to come, or that he *cannot* come. Is the first night guaranteed, meaning that you will pay for it whether it is occupied or not? If so, is the individual or your organization responsible for the payment? If you are guaranteeing the room, plan on making a decision whether to hold the room before the time when the charge will be made to your group.

MEETING ROOMS. Who has the authority to make changes in meeting or function room assignments or setups? This should be decided and made known well before the event, and in my opinion the authority should be as limited as possible. Have it limited either to one person or to a very few who can be trusted to stay in constant communication with each other. Failure to assign this authority can mean chaos for the hotel's conference staff and room setups that are inappropriate to the function. Likewise, it should be in writing that the hotel may not make any alterations to agreed details without prior notification and approval by you.

PERIPHERAL FUNCTIONS. What will you do if one (or more) of your group decides at the last minute to have a side meeting of a subset of your group? And what if there is a conflict between this subgroup and your function, or between two subgroups? What about sponsored hospitality suites? Do you have any control over these? If you can achieve it, you should get an agreement within your group that all such side meetings will be decided on no later than a set date (sometime before the conference and one that is comfortable to you) and, to avoid conflicts, that all such meetings will be approved by an appropriate official of your group. Although you cannot always prevent unofficial hospitality suites, you should at least get agreement from the hotel to notify you of such rentals, with times and dates, so you can discuss the events with the sponsors if it appears to conflict with, for example, your awards banquet.

MISSED HANDOUTS. This will happen too. Either the speaker forgot one (or more) or they got lost in shipment. Shipping problems can be minimized by agreeing on very specific shipping instructions and addresses and by choosing a shipper and shipping time that assures you of delivery on time and to a place where the materials will not be lost. For those missing handouts, whether lost or forgotten, have a plan for last-minute copying, either through the hotel or through a local fast print shop. If your budget is tight, you would be well advised to shop for the latter because hotel in-house printing services are usually slow and almost always exorbitantly expensive. With a very few exceptions, they are designed to discourage you from using the service because the hotel does not want to run a print shop.

WEATHER. How can you control the weather? Well, of course, you can't, but you can make plans in case. First, you can check the weather patterns for your chosen location during the time of your event. In some cases you can time your event for the most favorable weather season for your locale. Then you can make contingent plans for any event that can be affected by the weather. If you are planning a poolside cocktail party, have a contingent room where it can be placed in case of rain. If you plan a golf tournament, either plan an alternative activity or at least make arrangements for refunds if you cannot play golf due to weather.

STRIKES. Once again, how can you know whether a strike will happen, and if one does, what can you do? Depending on the union and the makeup of your group, this may or may not present a problem. If a minor union in the hotel goes on strike, and other unions in the hotel do not honor the picket line, unless your group is a union, this may not mean anything to your function. On the other hand, a strike that closes the hotel one week before your convention can be a major disaster! Of course you could avoid union facilities, but this is not really a viable solution for many reasons. You can, however, inquire as to the status of the union contract during your negotiations and watch the papers as your conference time approaches to see whether labor storms are brewing. Also, almost all hotel contracts have clauses referring to contingencies in case of strike. Read them carefully, and know what your options are if something like a strike happens.

SPEAKER ILLNESS or illness by some other key member of the group. (Illnesses by meeting planners are not, of course, permitted.) If your keynote speaker doesn't show, what is the plan? It's not practical to have a pinchhitter on call in case of such an occurrence, but you should have a plan. Maybe there is a member of your group who can substitute, or maybe you will be better off if you just announce the illness and forget the speech. But know in advance what you will do, so you don't panic if it happens.

SPECIAL MEALS. This one often causes headaches, and it shouldn't, for two reasons. One, if you design your registration forms correctly, you can request registrants to identify any special meal needs when they register; and two, the hotel can almost always make a miraculous switch at the last minute to cater to your problem eater. Of course, when planning your meal events, you must be aware of any major group characteristics that dictate meal design. For example, you don't serve beef to the National Association of Vegetarians. Hotel magic only extends so far!

MEAL GUARANTEES. This is a last-minute task (usually 48 to 72 hours before the meal) and should remain so. But how to cope? There are several tools to use. First, check your latest registration figures, and try to anticipate any additional sign-ups between now and the meal. Second, anticipate some "no-shows", even if the meal is paid for. Better offers, illness, any number of reasons come up. So be conservative in your counts for meals, as you will have fewer for meals than you have registered. Third, the host facility will overset by a certain amount and will be prepared to serve more than your guarantee. Fourth, work out an arrangement with the hotel in case you miss the boat by a significant amount (say ten percent). Can they set more tables in a hurry while you provide free drinks to those who have to wait? If not, can they provide meals in their restaurant for those who cannot be seated? How will you compensate those who are not served? Or, if your budget allows and you don't want the hassle, go ahead and guarantee on the high side to make sure no one gets left out or otherwise offended. Be aware, if you take this course, that you will pay for the guaranteed number even if only half show up. So this can be an expensive insurance policy.

FUNCTION TIMING. The way to avoid functions running late and interfering with other events is to know your speakers and their propensities to "run on". Schedule the long-winded ones where they can't make a problem. Put them last for the day rather than in the morning. Then make sure you allow ample time between when they are supposed to end and when the first evening function begins. Realistically, of course, you don't always have either this knowledge or this power. If you have concurrent workshops, which need to end at the same time, you need to tell workshop leaders that you will be calling time on them perhaps ten or fifteen minutes before they are to conclude. If the coffee service is ready before the speaker is ready to break, will the coffee stay warm? Will the Danish do the same? If you know there may be delays, the hotel can assist by providing your service on warming trays or coffee urns with burners beneath.

Another thing to remember in avoiding overlapping events is to allow more time than you think you need between events, at least fifteen minutes if they are in the same area of the hotel. Overloaded agendas are the downfall of many meetings. Remember the last time you got stuck behind a group of people when trying to walk down a hallway? It can take forever to move a group from a session room to a ballroom. And of course if there is travel involved, say across town, plan on it taking longer than you think it will, both because of traffic and because several people will find it necessary to be "stylishly late" getting on the bus.

LOST REGISTRATION FEES. Some people arrive knowing that they sent in their check, but you have no record of that. What will you do? Turn them away, take their word for it and hope their checks show up, or hit some other happy medium? What about badges and rooms for these people? (You might as well add on-site registrants to this scenario because they require the same kinds of decisions, and they will happen, unless you specifically forbid them.) The key here is not what you do, because that may vary depending on the importance of the individual, the nature of the event, how badly you need their attendance, or how much grief their acceptance will cause. What *is* important is that you know what should be done and make this known to your registration table personnel so that when it happens the solution is an easy one, not a major crisis requiring your personal intervention when you already are involved in another crisis that could have been anticipated.

We could go on with other examples and ideas of how to cope with the situation, but the point, I hope, is made. *Anticipation*, and only that, will keep you from having to deal with unplanned and potentially damaging last-minute issues at your conference.

On-Site Management

▷ Well, after all the months of planning, organizing, anticipating and other work involved with meeting planning, it's finally time for your conference. So what is your role during the actual conference? Basically it is to be on-site early, to stay late, and to be everywhere before anybody else is. It sounds impossible, but it really isn't all that hard. Depending on the size of your conference, you may have to delegate some of your on-site management to assistants, but you are ultimately responsible for seeing to it that all planned activities occur as you planned them. To do this, I recommend several steps, some of which were first described in an article I wrote for the newsletter *Meeting Planners Alert*. They are as follows:

1. PRE-PLAN. As covered in the previous chapter, this means writing up a very detailed plan for each event, no matter how small. Even a board meeting of ten people needs a specific room setup, with perhaps some audio-visual equipment as well. Don't assume you can handle this from memory. Remember that

during the actual conference you may be checking on 20 to more than 100 room or function setups; so commit the plans to paper in advance to prevent confusion, to eliminate stress and to permit delegation to your staff of some inspection duties.

Some meeting planners feel that this detailed checking is the responsibility of the facility's conference coordinating staff, and perhaps it is. Any professional convention manager will have a detailed function sheet detailing all the things that the hotel staff are supposed to do to service your meeting. Unfortunately, however, these come in so many different designs and use so many different methods of conveying information that it is difficult sometimes for you to follow. You should obtain this function sheet before you arrive at the conference and check it over. It will probably even be useful to you in preparing your own checklist. Don't allow it to substitute for your list though. It will list only what the hotel staff are to do, not the things you have to remember. Also, who will get the blame if something goes wrong? Don't assume that nothing will go wrong. Maybe it won't, and you can be pleasantly surprised. But when something does go awry, if you have anticipated that possibility and are checking the situation early enough to allow correction, no harm will be done. How detailed your checklist is depends, among other things, on how many items you need to check and how experienced you are at doing these checks. I recently saw a checklist prepared by an inexperienced meeting manager that covered two pages, single-spaced. That was for one day's events *before* breakfast! Her entire week-long conference plan covered 65 pages. Nothing went wrong, however, that anyone other than the meeting manager noticed, so the work was worth it. A portion of a typical detailed plan is reproduced here to give you a flavor of the types of things you should record and check.

FRIDAY

6:00 A.M.
- Check to see apprenticeship room is ready. Bring sign and meeting materials

7:00–8:00 A.M.
- Apprenticeship Curriculum Review
  Convention center, Room 206
    15 participants, conference style flip chart, overhead projector, screen, 2 pots coffee, Sanka, tea, water (set in back of room)

7:00 A.M.
- Check exhibit hall for re-opening
- Call registration desk personnel
- Check exhibit signs
- Check breakfast setup and sponsor sign
- Breakfast is coffee, tea, Sanka, three juices,
- Danish, croissants, butter, sugar, cream, water
- Set up for 250, just inside exhibit hall entrance
- Check for discard trays, no ashtrays

7:15 A.M.
- Check registration desk setup
    2 tables, 4 chairs, coat rack, typewriter, badge holders, pencils, paper

7:45 A.M.
- Registration desk opens

8:00 A.M.
- Exhibit hall opens, breakfast begins

—and so it goes, until after midnight.

2. TIE DOWN PLANS. It is absolutely essential that you have a so-called "tie down" meeting, or preconference session with hotel staff to go over all of your plans in detail. All of the hotel's department heads should be in attendance for at least part of this meeting, so that everyone's role in the conference is understood by everyone else and the staff gets to know who you are and your helpers too (if you have any). It's important to put faces

with names, to find out numbers or "beeper codes" of key staff, and to know how to get in touch in case of a problem of any kind. Be prepared to cover not only planned, but unplanned, portions of your agenda. The facility will want to know, for example, when your Tuesday evening is empty, how many are expected to eat in the hotel's restaurant? This detail can mean the difference between efficient and inefficient restaurant service. If you are providing informal hospitality suites late in the evening, know what hotel rules or local ordinances the security officer is required to enforce. You don't need to have a confrontation between the hotel security officer and your inebriated CEO. Nor do you want your guests embarrassed by being asked to leave the swimming pool at 10:00 P.M.

3. HAVE A "PLAN B". Know in advance what to do when a breakdown occurs. Projector bulbs do burn out. What do you do? Whom do you call? If coffee is late, how do you cover and expedite at the same time? If the microphone starts to howl, where is the volume control so you can fix it? (Waiting for the engineer is not what to do here.)

4. DON'T GET INVOLVED. By this I mean do not try to be an active participant in the substance of the meeting. Your job is to work behind the scenes during event #1 to see that event #2 goes off without a hitch. You can't do this if you are on a panel as a participant. If you must take part in a session, appoint a substitute to fill your meeting planner role.

5. COME EARLY, STAY LATE. I have said this already. It bears repeating. What it means is that you must arrive at the conference at least a day, maybe more, ahead of others and stay until at least all official departures have occurred and all bills reviewed.

When you arrive, look around. Of course you have already done a site inspection, but that may have been months, or even years, earlier. Check to see what's on the reader board in the lobby. What other groups are actually in house, as opposed to what you were told? Watch activities at the front desk. Is the staff handling requests as you would like to see your group's requests handled? If not, speak to the front desk manager now, not after you get complaints. If check-outs are proceeding, are they being done efficiently? If not, can you suggest a change that will help your group check out when it's time?

Walk through the property, preferably on your own. Check the hours of the restaurants, the pool, the health club, the bar. Are any adjustments needed to suit your group? If another meeting is going on, check the coffee service. Is it what you want for your group, or will changes be needed?

Look for your materials. Don't just take someone's word for it that "all have arrived." Have a shipping list with you, and physically identify each box you shipped, and arrange for delivery to appropriate spots within the hotel at certain times.

If possible, preregister your VIPs, and get their room keys to spare their standing in line on arrival.

Come early also means come early to each event (or have someone do it for you). Don't arrive at the opening session 15 minutes before it is to begin. If you get there at least an hour ahead any necessary changes can be made without panic. Check the microphone(s), overhead projectors, lighting, heat controls, magic markers. Check the glasses; are they clean?

Check the reader board each morning to see that your events are properly listed and directed and to see again who else is doing what in the hotel.

Check the placement of the bars at your cocktail party. Are they properly spaced to disperse traffic, or will they create bottlenecks?

It is critical to the success of this prechecking that the hotel or other facility knows you'll be doing it and when. If you inspect two hours before a function, and they don't plan to complete setup until 30 minutes prior to the function, some adjustment is needed. You must also make it known that your checking does not mean you don't trust them. The reason for your extra caution is to make sure that both you and they look good.

6. KNOW WHAT YOU WANT/NEED, AND STICK TO IT. There will always be at least one, usually several more, who think they know more than you do about how to set up a room, place a microphone, or set room temperature. You are in charge, and you must remain in charge. Of course the meeting room will seem too cold to the early arrivals: it will warm up soon with the arrival of numerous warm bodies. Don't overreact to the freezing early arrival, or you'll end up with a superheated room.

Sometimes plans or setups have to change. Maybe the speaker forgot to tell you that he or she intended to use slides. If you can, you magically produce a slide projector. You have to review each request in light of the entire agenda and the function's purpose. Because you will be held responsible for the success of the function, you may need to use your authority to exercise that responsibility. Again, make sure the hotel staff knows to respond only to those who have authority to make changes.

7. CENTRALIZE THE FOCUS ON YOU. You should make yourself known to both the hotel and your participants as the one to whom all problems should be addressed. I know that sounds like asking for trouble, but that's your job. If someone has a problem with a room rate, it could be an isolated or a general issue. If it's general, you need to know so you can fix it before others encounter the same problem. If it's isolated, you will be able to fix it more easily than the participant can, because you are recognized by the hotel staff as being a person with

authority. Incidentally, it doesn't hurt to identify yourself as someone who is both willing to help and to take responsibility for success of the meeting. (It will be a success, won't it?)

8. CHECK CONSUMPTION COUNTS. You should be checking continually on consumption counts during your conference. After each break, dinner or cocktail party, do your own counts. In some cases, such as parties where you are paying for liquor by the bottle, you may want to do a limited count during the function, by watching from time to time to see that bottles are emptied before others are opened. With a few exceptions you pay for opened bottles whether consumed or not. At coffee breaks you often pay for soft drinks by consumption. But who is counting? Are you paying for actual consumption or for what was put out?

Another reason for checking consumption is to adjust amounts ordered for future functions. Though you have to guarantee at least two days ahead of time, you might be able to save money by adjusting the number of doughnuts or gallons of coffee served on day three based on consumption on day one. Or if the mix is wrong, say between doughnuts and Danish, and all the Danish go and the doughnuts are left, you can save money if you "ditch the doughnuts" and add more Danish.

At meals, you can count places set before the dinner, then check during the dinner to see how many places are empty. This doesn't take long, can be done inconspicuously, and assures that you don't pay for more than your guarantee or number actually served, (whichever is greater).

I once observed during a dinner dance a practice that could have been stopped on the spot. Drinks were being sold by the drink, but every time someone got up to dance the glass disappeared, whether the drink was finished or not. This is both costly and aggravating to your guests and need not be tolerated. I have also observed waiters hiding wine bottles behind drapes for their own consumption later on. In this latter case the catering manager was notified and immediate adjustments (and probably some firings) took place. Such things happen very rarely, but the fact that they can occur underscores your need to be on the alert.

I did make a point about not getting involved under point #4. You don't want to be an outsider who doesn't participate at all in the party both because it's boring to be just an observer and because you don't want to look like a security officer or chaperone. However, everything in moderation. While partying, remember to keep your first priority in mind. One thing I suggest is that you do not sign bills during a function but have them delivered to your room or conference office nightly. It's better to check them in private and at your own pace rather than to give them a cursory look while carrying on a conversation or listening to a speaker.

9. HAVE FUN. Final point. While this may seem ridiculous given all the duties I have dumped on you, you should try to enjoy yourself. You've worked hard enough to bring this event off, you deserve to enjoy it too. Even more important, having made yourself somewhat a center of attention by being in charge, it behooves you to at least appear to be having a good time. This event may be the highlight of the year for many of your participants. You will enhance their enjoyment if they are convinced that you feel things are going well. Never, never, never, tell others about a problem you solved during the conference. If they didn't see it, it didn't happen. This does not mean you shouldn't point it out to the boss after the conference. Too much modesty will get you no promotions or other recognition you deserve. But your participants should feel it is a perfect meeting because you're smiling, not frowning. Enjoy your success!

18

Billing and Payment

Finally comes the time to pay the bills, the last act in your production of a successful conference. If you have taken most of the steps I recommended earlier, you shouldn't have too much trouble at this point. Everything you expect to pay should be known to you, and you will already have seen itemized bills for each event as it occurred.

Nevertheless, there are some things you should do while still on-site to make sure there are as few misunderstandings or hassles as possible. In most cases the final bill will be sent to you after you leave. However, if you request it, you should be able to sit down with the people in the accounting office before you leave and find out what they think will be included in the bill. It is amazing to me how difficult it seems to be for sales people to communicate with accounting people. You can come across some very strange charges, and it's better to clear them up while you can still talk face-to-face with people. You may need to get sales, catering and accounting people all in the same room at the same time. Here are a few things to look for.

SLEEPING ROOMS. In most cases the sleeping room charges will be paid by individuals who attended your conference. In some instances, as we've noted, you may be paying for these as part of the master bill. If so, check to see if the check-in, check-out pattern for each guest agrees with yours. If not, correct it now. If the hotel has missed a room or two, don't try to hide it or "get away" without paying for it. It will turn up later and create hard feelings. If you used the room, tell them, and pay for it. Your reputation will be known before you sign your next contract, so make sure it's a good one. By the same token, if you didn't use the room, don't pay for it. Are the people listed all yours, or was some outsider mistakenly billed to your group? Are there charges for hospitality suites that should have been billed to other sponsors?

What was your agreement about guaranteeing for "no-shows"? Were you to be billed for one night or for the entire scheduled length of stay? Which are you being billed for?

Are your complimentary rooms properly credited? What was the method used to calculate your complimentary block? Was it rooms per night, or total rooms for the conference? If the latter, did your early arrivals and late departures get included in the totals?

Even if you are not paying for rooms, you may still find some room charges on your bill. It's possible that one or more of your group checked out without paying, either inadvertently or on purpose. If so, that will be on your bill, if not now, then eventually. Also, check for incidental charges such as room service or telephone charges. Whether paying for rooms on the master bill or not, these charges are normally handled separately. If there was a disagreement about some of these incidental charges, and one of your participants refused to pay for them, you should not be liable unless you agreed in advance to cover such items. That disagreement is between the hotel and the guest.

There is no way you can know who is right, so you shouldn't be involved.

BANQUET AND OTHER FUNCTION CHARGES. Check the counts and charges for food served at the banquet and other similar functions. They should, of course, agree with the itemized sheets you saw earlier. How are taxes being handled? This is where the infamous "plus-plus" comes into play. The normal procedure is for hotels to add a charge for gratuities to the meal price, say 17 percent, plus a tax of perhaps 8 percent. This means you are paying tax on gratuities. Check the state laws before you get to this point (in fact during negotiations) and know your rights. Depending on state law, and sometimes on the way in which gratuities are distributed, you may not have to pay this tax on tips.

LAST MINUTE CHARGES. Check for charges on such things as copying, telephone charges and special labor fees. It could be that while the salesperson told you the copy charges would be waived, somehow the internal accounting mechanism ended up charging you $.25 per page for that two-page handout you needed 100 copies of. That's only $50, but why pay it if you needn't? And because it's so small, unless you get it straightened out now, the salesperson will not remember. (Or, if it's more than a month before you get the bill, the salesperson is liable to be gone, leaving you dead in the water.)

PACKAGE PRICES. Check to make sure that what was to have been included in any package price you negotiated was in fact included and not billed separately. More than once I have received this rude surprise. In one case all coffee breaks were to be included in the sleeping room rate, but they were billed separately, even though the sleeping room rate charged was high enough to cover them. Because the salesperson had moved on between the time of negotiation and the time I got the bill, it took me nine months before the bill finally got straightened out. In another example, Sunday brunch was to be hosted by the hotel but ended up being charged to me. This time, because the catering manager was on-site, and I caught the error before I left, the correction was made.

RIGHT BILL, WRONG WORDING. In some cases, you know what event is being billed, and you agree with the amount, but you know the bill will not be paid by your agency, boss, or board, unless the wording is changed. Just two examples to explain what I mean. Case one involved a meeting held in the parlor of a suite. The group was small, the suite had a very nice conference table, and everything was above-board and very business-like. The charges incurred were for morning and afternoon coffee breaks. But because it was delivered to a suite, it was charged as "Room Service" and against the account of the meeting leader, who was occupying the room adjacent to the parlor. No one in Accounting at this firm would have agreed to pay for Mr. X's room service charges, so the bill had to be reworded.

Case two involved a dinner for which we had agreed to cut the portion size of the entree in order to include wine with the dinner. (See Chapter 7.) The bill separately identified wine, and that, for this association, was a definite red flag. So Sales had to talk to Accounting, which as I have said is not easy, to get them to change the bill.

PAYMENT DETAILS. Finally, after all the bills and wording have been agreed to, what are the details of how you are expected to pay? Did you make a deposit on the meeting? If so, was it credited? Do you earn a discount by paying within 10 or 30 days, and is there a penalty for delayed payment? Suppose a portion of the bill is going to remain under question for a period of time, but the rest of the bill is fine. Should you pay the uncontested portion to avoid interest charges, or can you use this unpaid bill as "clout" to force a quick settlement of the disputed portion of the bill? All these details should be spelled out in your contract and should be adhered to, to avoid any unpleasant surprises.

Finally, an appeal to fair play. If the contract does not specify any penalty for late payment, but you know you owe the bill and you have the money to pay it, please do. Remember that we are in the hospitality industry and that hospitality should extend to both sides. If the hotel people performed as you contracted for, they have a right to prompt and full payment.

Conference Evaluation

▷ Let us assume, for the sake of this chapter, that you have now survived your conference in good order. That assumption is necessary, because if you didn't, you don't have to do an evaluation. I contend that you should do an evaluation of your conference experience, both to judge your success and to improve future similar functions. But how do you evaluate yourself? Everyone says evaluation is good, but in my experience (except for training meetings) conferences are rarely evaluated at all. When they are, the evaluation sheets are not well designed and are incomplete.

Perhaps the most common form of evaluation is what I call the "smile index". You simply ask participants to rate their experience at the conference, sometimes on a scale of 1 to 10, sometimes in a narrative format. While this information is useful, it is not enough. It is not the most important evaluation to make.

PARTICIPANT REACTIONS

The evaluation can either be done anonymously, which supposedly gives you a more honest opinion, or you can request signatures, which has an advantage if certain participants' comments mean more than others. The problem with the anonymous evaluation is that you have no idea who did not complete one; it doesn't tell how accurately the responses reflect the feelings of the entire group, or of some subset of the group. Scales of 1 to 10 sound like a good idea at first, especially if you go so far as to designate, for example, that 1–3 means poor, 4–6 average, and 7–10 excellent. You still don't know what excellent means to me as opposed to my neighbor. Nor does the scale tell why something was excellent or poor.

In general I value narrative comments more than scores, but they leave me wondering whether those who make the effort to write some words represent the group. Am I hearing only from the "lunatic fringe" who are either greatly happy or greatly angry (or both)?

You can attempt to eliminate the problem of partial response by somehow requiring an evaluation before the participants leave (put guards at the exit door?), but I seriously doubt whether this does you any good. An unfortunate aspect of most evaluations is that they are to be completed at the end of the conference, when the primary interest or focus is preparing to leave.

Another problem with these evaluations is that they measure attitude, which is only part of the measurement. You may feel great after a particular lecture because it was funny. But when the euphoria wears off, you may realize you gained nothing except laughter from listening to this speaker; no new information was provided. Also, we all come to a situation with a certain preset, which can unfairly influence our recall of a certain function. As an example, if I had to sit next to a real jerk at dinner, I may remember the dinner as terrible, regardless of what I ate. If I rate the dinner as "poor", you won't know why because I may not honestly remember why.

With all these caveats and problems, however, I still advocate doing some form of evaluation by your conference participants of how they feel. After all, they are in a certain sense your customers, and especially if attendance is voluntary, their return to future conferences will in part depend on how they felt about this one. I have two suggestions to make here.

1) Try to make the questions non-leading, and include a chance for negative as well as positive comments. I sometimes use a simple three-question format which goes like this:
 a. What were the strengths of this conference?
 b. What were the weaknesses of this conference?
 c. What suggestions do you have for future conferences?

2) Try not to read the evaluations until you have a chance to rest from the conference and reflect for yourself how you feel about it. If you read them too soon, you may overreact to any negatives, and tend to discount them. Remember that when you are tired, you automatically feel defensive (after all it was your best effort). Also, the positives won't offset as they should, because negatives are stronger when we are tired.

ACHIEVING OBJECTIVES

Other than the "smile index", what should you or can you do to evaluate the conference? If you recall, I emphasized at the start how vital it is to set conference or meeting objectives before you begin. If you have done this, go back and look at them, and ask yourself whether we accomplished them. If you did, at least in some way you have succeeded. If not, no matter how happy your participants are, at least to a degree you failed. Of course it follows that the more objectively measurable your goals are the more easily you can tell whether you met them.

I also said that it is important to define the real, as opposed to the politically acceptable, meeting goals. Thus, if you really only wanted to have a get-together, but you had to make up a reason for the meeting in order to get budget approval, then worry about the get-together, not whether you met the phony goals you published for budget purposes.

EVALUATE PROCESS

Finally, you should evaluate the process of putting the meeting together. How did you do? Particularly in Chapter 6 (Budgeting) and in Chapter 11 (Materials Development) we discussed developing plans for success, including recording both planned and actual dates for accomplishing different tasks. This idea of examining your processes and procedures permeates several other aspects of planning as well, including negotiations, site selection, etc. Were your budget estimates close, or did you miss some major cost or income factor? When you set up timelines for materials development were you accurate, or did you find yourself in a time crunch at one or more points in the process? In site selection, you probably made a judgment that factor A in some hotel was more important than factor B in another. Did this prove to be true, or did none of your group in fact care a whit about factor A? (Golf course, as an example, versus tennis courts.) In travel logistics you made certain assumptions. Were they correct?

By going over each step of the plan you both explicitly and implicitly developed, and checking to see whether (or more likely where) you made errors or forgot to factor in a consideration, you can make your job easier next time. You can also improve future conferences, thus ever raising your personal star while benefiting your company, association or other organization.

A NOTE TO MEETING AND PARTY PLANNERS

If you would like to order additional copies of MEETING MANAGEMENT, please use order form on following page. These other EPM books on Washington subjects make excellent references and/or presentation gifts and indispensable references:

UNIQUE MEETING PLACES IN GREATER WASHINGTON. No other book ever made a meeting or party planner's work so easy. Nearly 100 special, rentable sites—grand halls, old inns, museums, famous homes—are described in colorful detail, with capacities, rates, catering arrangements. $12.95

WALKING TOURS OF OLD WASHINGTON AND ALEXANDRIA. $100,000 might buy you the original Paul Hogarth watercolors reproduced here in full color, but then you'd be missing the engaging text and the convenience of taking it all along as you step back into the distinguished heritage preserved in our capital's finest old buildings. Usable art; exquisite gift. $8\frac{1}{2} \times 11$. $24.95

FOOTNOTE WASHINGTON. Bryson Rash, one of Washington's most beloved broadcasters, takes readers down the engaging, humorous and surprising bypaths of capital history. Inspired by President Truman's tale of a sex change on an equestrian statue, this is not the most important book ever to come out of Washington, but certainly the most entertaining. Illustrated. $8.95

THE WALKER WASHINGTON GUIDE. The sixth edition of the "guide's guide to Washington," completely revised by Katharine Walker, builds on a 25-year reputation as the top general guide to the capital. Its 320 pages are packed with museums, galleries, hotels, restaurants, theaters, shops, churches, as well as sights. Beautiful maps and photos. Indispensable. $7.95

MR. LINCOLN'S CITY. For any Civil War buff. Hidden among the impressive buildings and landscaped lawns of modern Washington are innumerable reminders of the tumultuous years 1861–1865. This engrossing guide to those historic sites doubles as illustrated history, with 130 photographs and 15 excellent maps. $8\frac{1}{2} \times 11$. $17.95

MILESTONES INTO HEADSTONES. These mini biographies of 50 fascinating Americans buried in Washington are loaded with entertaining anecdotes. Find out why Abner Doubleday has been benched as baseball's inventor, how Peggy Eaton caused Andrew Jackson's entire cabinet to resign, and why John Philip Sousa became a tobacco pitchman. 40 photographs. $9.95

OLD ALEXANDRIA. The most complete and authoritative guide to George Washington's hometown, offering walking tours as well as delightfully readable, carefully researched history of this old port. Along streets that retain their 18th-century charm stand dozens of American architectural and cultural gems; OLD ALEXANDRIA takes you there. 65 photographs. $9.95

ONE-DAY TRIPS THROUGH HISTORY. An unusual guide to 200 historic sites within 150 miles of Washington, this collection is favored by visitors and residents alike. Arranged chronologically starting with prehistory, the site descriptions give you a chance to brush up on your history while having a pleasant day's outing with children or out-of-town guests. $9.95

The form below can be used for orders of fewer than ten books. For retailer quantity discounts, please write us or call 1-800-289-2339.

ORDER BLANK. Mail with check to:
EPM Publications, Box 490, McLean, VA 22101

Title	Qty	Price	Amount
_____	____	_____	_____
_____	____	_____	_____
_____	____	_____	_____

Subtotal _____

Virginia residents add 4½% tax _____

Orders totalling up to $15 add $2 shipping/handling _____

Orders totalling more than $15 add $3 first item, $1 ea. add'l. _____

Total _____

Name _____

Street _____

City _____ State _____ Zip _____

Remember to enclose names, addresses and enclosure cards for gift purchases.
Prices are subject to change. Write or call for free catalog: 1-800-289-2339.

About the Author

RANDY TALBOT, a native Californian, wrote MEETING MANAGEMENT from 20 years of experience in planning meetings and conferences for the Bureau of Labor Statistics in Washington, D.C. He is the founding President of the Society of Government Meeting Planners (SGMP) and speaks on various aspects of the meeting profession to industry audiences such as the Hotel Sales and Management chapters.

He writes many articles for trade press magazines, advises a trade newsletter, and teaches seminars on meeting management. He participates with his wife, Julie, in Talbot Site Seminars (TSS), a firm devoted to teaching about meetings and site selection. TSS has conducted more than 30 familiarization trips for meeting planners in the last four years. In addition to planning approximately 70 meetings a year, Randy makes time for traveling, antique collecting, and his prize-winning photography. He and his wife have two daughters.